WHAT'S THE DEAL WITH DEAL WITH DEAD MAN'S CURVE?
AND OTHER
REALLY GOOD QUESTIONS
ABOUT
CLEVELAND

WHAT'S THE DEAL WITH DEAD MAN'S CURVE?

AND OTHER
REALLY GOOD QUESTIONS
ABOUT
CLEVELAND

JIM SWEENEY

GRAY & COMPANY, PUBLISHERS
CLEVELAND

Gray & Company, Publishers
www.grayco.com

ISBN 978-1-59851-131-4
Printed in the United States of America
1

Contents

WHAT'S THE DEAL WITH DEAD MAN'S CURVE?
AND OTHER
REALLY GOOD QUESTIONS
ABOUT
CLEVELAND

Introduction

Cleveland is not the city it used to be.

It's not as big, not as important, not as wealthy as it was in the 1930s, when it was the sixth-largest city in the country.

Beginning in the 1950s, it went through decades of decline, became a national punchline, and then underwent a rebirth of sorts in the 1980s. Since then, it's been labeled a Comeback City (more than once) and has made its way onto various Best and Worst lists. It has failed to overcome many of the problems that sent it into decline, but it has found other ways to progress.

It's OK that Cleveland isn't what it once was.

Age and decline bring character. Old cities are fascinating in the same way that pictures of Keith Richards are. Both landscapes are wrinkled and pocked, full of fissures and folds. Both reward closer examination.

Cities past their prime are full of forgotten corners and objects that have outlived their original purpose. And, unlike in some faster-growing cities, these quirks are not always paved over to make room for newer, shinier things.

Do you think Arlington, Texas, or Mesa, Arizona, both of which are newer and more populous than Cleveland, have a fraction of this city's character, quirks, and mysteries? Not a chance. They're just overgrown suburbs of Dallas and Phoenix.

But things do get forgotten along the way. Something that made perfect sense one hundred years ago now leaves people wondering about its purpose. The reasons why something is *this* way and not *that* way are forgotten. How certain things came about is lost.

Ask a local about these mysteries and you'll get either an explanation, sometimes accurate, sometimes not, or a shrug and, "I dunno. It's always been like that."

This book answers some of those questions about Cleveland. It delves into the whys and the long-ago decisions, forces, and circumstances that shaped the city. It explores why some things about Cleveland have changed and why others haven't—and probably never will.

Finding out why things are the way they are is a means to understanding a city, from its beginnings to its current state. It can also be a way to figure out how to alter the things that need to change and how to save those that should be preserved.

It's my hope that this book will help explain Cleveland to long-term residents and newcomers alike and give them a deeper understanding of where they live.

Thanks for reading.

Why Did the Cuyahoga River Burn?

If there's one stigma that Cleveland has battled more than any other, it's the fact that its river caught fire.

A waterway so polluted it could burn seemed the perfect punchline for Cleveland of the 1970s: a city considered wretched, dirty, and hopeless.

The June 2, 1969, fire on the Cuyahoga River made headlines around the world. And by all accounts, it was a pretty spectacular blaze as burning waterways go. Flames reached as high as five stories before the conflagration was brought under control by a fireboat and three fire battalions fighting it from the shore.

A bridge belonging to the Norfolk & Western Railway Co. sustained $45,000 in damage and was forced to close for repairs. A Newburgh & South Shore Railroad Co. trestle also was damaged but remained open.

The apparent cause was an accumulation of oily waste and wooden debris clumped around the trestles at the foot of the Campbell Road hill.

According to a subsequent investigation by Cleveland's Bureau of Industrial Wastes, the fire probably came from a discharge of highly volatile petroleum derivatives and was ignited by a spark from a train passing overhead.

Of course, this was not the first time the Cuyahoga had caught fire, nor was it even the worst blaze. The river had burned at least a dozen times previously, dating back to the 1800s. A 1952 fire caused $1.5 million in damages; a 1912 blaze killed five people. Fire was simply a hazard that came with treating the river as a combination sewer, industrial waste dump, and watery commercial highway.

To be fair, the Cuyahoga River was not the only polluted waterway to catch fire. The Chicago River, River Rouge in Detroit, and the Buffalo River also burned at various times around the same period.

But singer/songwriter Randy Newman didn't write a song about those fires. It was the Cuyahoga River fire that inspired his 1972 release, "Burn On," which contained the lines:

> Cleveland, even now I can remember
> Cause the Cuyahoga River
> Goes smokin' through my dreams

A history of neglect

The befouling of the Cuyahoga River began almost as soon as White people settled along its banks. In addition to providing transportation and water, the river was a natural sewer, absorbing whatever was dumped into it and carrying it away—if not all the way to the lake, then at least out of sight.

That negligence quickly took its toll. Consider this description of the river from an immigrant in the 1880s:

> Yellowish-black rings of oil circled on its surface like grease in soup. The water was yellowish, thick, full of clay, stinking of oil and sewage. Piles of rotting wood were heaped on either bank of the river, and it was all dirty and neglected.

Rennselaer Herrick, who was mayor from 1879 to 1882, called it "a sewer that runs through the heart of the city."

The composition of the pollution changed over the decades, from slaughterhouse offal and tannery waste to oil spills, acid runoff from steel mills, and partially treated sewage from Cleveland, Akron, and the cities in between. No matter how foul it got, though, it was never really seen as a civic problem until the 1960s. And then it went national.

The Cuyahoga River burned on November 1, 1952. It wasn't the first time, and it wouldn't be the last. *Cleveland Press*

Sparking a movement

The 1969 fire came at a time when the environmental movement was gaining strength and awareness of the cost of pollution was growing. A *Time* magazine article covered the fire and, as a result, the dirty Cuyahoga and filthy Lake Erie became national symbols of pollution. (*Time* staffers apparently couldn't find a picture of the 1969 fire, so they ran a shot of the much bigger 1952 blaze.)

Cleveland mayor Carl Stokes, who had taken office in 1968, was one of the first politicians to recognize the damage pollution does to a city and its residents. As the first elected Black mayor of a major U.S. city, Stokes was already news, and his activism helped raise awareness of the problem.

In November 1968, city residents approved a bond issue to clean up the river and lake by improving the sewer system.

The day after the 1969 fire, Stokes held a press conference on the banks of the Cuyahoga and vowed to clean it up.

The blaze became a turning point in the environmental movement. Inspired by the fire, Congress later that year passed the National Environmental Policy Act, which established the U.S. Environmental Protection Agency. Congress in 1972 passed the Clean Water Act, which mandated cleanups of polluted rivers like the Cuyahoga.

The Cuyahoga fire and a disastrous oil spill off the coast of Santa Barbara, California, were also the impetus for an April 1970 environmental "teach-in" at college campuses. The annual event eventually became Earth Day.

A new flow

The Cuyahoga River and Lake Erie have come a long way since 1969. Kayakers and paddleboarders now float through Cleveland's Flats on currents once choked with sludge and debris. Water quality is on the rise. There is still much work to be done, though. Invasive species such as zebra mussels and gobies, as well as algae blooms fed by farm runoff, continue to threaten water quality.

But with progress being made, Clevelanders became comfortable embracing the slur. The Burning River name has been attached to everything from a local microbrew and roller derby league to a coffee shop and environmental festival.

The Cuyahoga's record of fifty years without a fire ended in 2020, though this time it wasn't because the river was dirty. A fuel tanker caught fire on Route 8 in Summit County, and the burning fuel ran into storm sewers that empty into the Cuyahoga in the Gorge Metroparks. That fire was quickly extinguished—and no jokes were made.

Why Didn't Moses Cleaveland Live in Cleveland?

The joke almost writes itself: Cleveland is so bad that its founder left and never came back.

There is an element of truth to it. Cleveland was founded by General Moses Cleaveland in the summer of 1796. And a few months later, he left, never to return.

Why go to all the trouble of founding a city only to abandon it?

The Connecticut connection

Ohio once belonged to Connecticut. Given the distance between the two states it now sounds ridiculous, but in the late 1700s Ohio was not yet a state. Connecticut, like many of the original thirteen colonies, had claims on unsettled western lands. In this case, Connecticut, under the terms of its charter, had been granted the rights to what is now Northeast Ohio by England's King Charles II.

Connecticut relinquished some of its western lands to the United States federal government in 1786 following the Revolutionary War and preceding the 1787 establishment of the Northwest Territory. It later sold much of its remaining "Western Reserve" to the Connecticut Land Company, a private firm that intended to sell parcels to settlers.

But before the Connecticut Land Company could sell the land, it had to survey it. So it hired Moses Cleaveland, a company director, attorney, and Revolutionary War veteran, to do the job.

In June 1796, Cleaveland set out from Schenectady, New York, at the head of a fifty-person expedition. Some traveled by land with horses and cattle, while the main body went in boats up the Mohawk River, down the Oswego River, along the southern shore of Lake Ontario, and up the Niagara River, portaging around Niagara Falls.

The expedition was halted briefly at Buffalo when a delegation of Mohawk and Seneca tribe members barred the way. The Native Americans stepped aside after receiving gifts valued at $1,200. The expedition sailed along the southern shore of Lake Erie and landed at the mouth of what is now known as Conneaut Creek on July 4, 1796, which they named Port Independence. Again, they placated local tribes with beads and whiskey in order to be allowed to proceed.

General Cleaveland skirted the shore with a surveying party and landed at the mouth of the Cuyahoga River on July 22, 1796. He decided the land on the eastern bluffs above the lake and river would be an ideal location for a city. He had it surveyed into town lots, and his employees named it Cleaveland in his honor.

The general and most of the expedition departed that October, leaving behind only a small group of settlers. Upon his return to New England, Cleaveland wrote:

> While I was in New Connecticut I laid out a town on the bank of Lake Erie, which was called by my name, and I believe the child is now born that may live to see that place as large as Old Windham.

The fact is that Cleaveland never set out to become a homesteading pioneer or to build a city. He was hired to do a surveying job, which he did, then returned home.

The real settlers

Other people deserve at least as much credit as Cleaveland for founding the new community.

Schoolteachers Job Phelps Stiles and his wife, Talitha, were two of the original settlers who stayed after Cleaveland left. In 1797, Talitha gave birth to Charles Phelps Stiles, the first White child born

Gen. Moses Cleaveland. He came, he surveyed, he left. *Cleveland Public Library*

in the Western Reserve. They lived at first on Lot 53, the present corner of West 3rd Street adjacent to the Terminal Tower, but later moved southeast to higher ground in Newburgh to escape malarial conditions in the lower Cuyahoga Valley.

The village of Cleaveland was incorporated on December 23, 1814. Its most memorable early citizen was Lorenzo Carter, another Connecticut native, who arrived in 1797. He built a large log cabin on the east bank of the Cuyahoga River—a replica stands there today—and later built the community's first tavern.

As for Moses Cleaveland, he never returned to Ohio, and in 1806, he died in Connecticut. In 1888, the Early Settlers Association of the Western Reserve erected a statue of the general in the southwest quadrant of Public Square, which Cleaveland's surveyors had laid out. The statue still stands, a presence far outlasting that of its namesake.

What happened to the missing A?

But why would a city so determined to honor its absent founder change the spelling of its name?

The story goes that an early city newspaper, the *Cleveland Advertiser*, changed the spelling in 1831 to make the name fit on its masthead. So that readers wouldn't think it was a mistake, the paper announced the change on its front page, calling the omitted (and silent) "a" superfluous. Other papers followed suit, and the city, when it incorporated in 1836, chose the popular spelling.

Actually, the "a" had gone missing before the *Advertiser*'s change. The city was spelled "Cleveland" on several of the maps prepared by Cleaveland's own surveyors. The general apparently didn't notice or, if he did, didn't object.

Though Connecticut no longer has any claims on Northeast Ohio, the phrase "Western Reserve" lives on in such institutions as Case Western Reserve University, Western Reserve Academy, Hospice of the Western Reserve, and Western Reserve Historical Society.

Cleveland, by the way, is a popular name for cities and towns—there are twenty-eight Clevelands in the U.S.—though only the one in Ohio was named for the general.

Why Do Clevelanders Wear So Many Cleveland T-shirts?

Want to know how Greater Clevelanders feel about their city? Don't bother asking them; just read their chests:

CLELAND THAT I LOVE

CLEVELAND AGAINST THE WORLD

BELIEVELAND

DEFEND CLEVELAND

And if the T-shirts aren't announcing the wearer's love for Cleveland, they're expressing similar affection for Ohio.

Go to any local flea market and it seems half the booths are selling Cleveland or Ohio gear. Any event from a Guardians game to a Blossom Music Center concert resembles a Cleveland-wear fashion show.

It's not the first moment for Cleveland-themed tees. In the late 1970s, a lot of residents donned *Cleveland: You Gotta Be Tough* and *Cleveland: Default's Not Mine* T-shirts, while every young adult owned at least three WMMS Buzzard shirts in honor of the power-house radio station. But those shirts didn't have the same booster message as the new ones.

Why do Greater Clevelanders feel such a need to proclaim their feelings for their city on their shirts?

Mike Kubinski, owner of CLE Clothing Co., says it has to do with a genuine love of the city. His decision to start the company in 2008 coincided with a surge in civic pride. Unlike the sarcastic, defensive spirit they showed in the 1970s, Clevelanders were

Cleveland Clothing Co.

taking genuine pride in where they live, and they wanted the world to know it.

"People really like this town, and they want to put it out there," he said.

CLE Clothing Co. has multiple brick-and-mortar shops as well as an online business. According to Kubinski, a lot of his customers are repeats, buying up new designs built around the same message: *I Liked Cleveland Before It Was Cool.*

How long will the fashion trend last? Kubinski doesn't see an end to it—not as long as Clevelanders still love their city.

What's the Deal with Dead Man's Curve?

Imagine what goes through the heads of unsuspecting truckers as they approach Dead Man's Curve on Interstate 90 in downtown Cleveland:

"Rumble strips? And why are those enormous signs warning me to slow down to 35 mph? The only reason I'd have to drive that slow would be a 90-degree curve ahead, and no one would be stupid enough to design an interstate with a curve that sharp . . . *OHMIGOD!*"

Since its opening in 1959, the stretch of I-90 just east of downtown has been surprising unsuspecting drivers who have been conditioned by good engineering and common sense to expect gradual curves on highways.

Though Dead Man's Curve isn't as deadly as its nickname implies, there have been more than fifteen fatal accidents there, and it causes nonfatal accidents on a regular basis, particularly overturned trucks, which can choke traffic into and out of downtown.

It used to be worse

The curve wasn't designed to be that bad. The original plan was for the interchange between the Shoreway and the Innerbelt to be a conventional cloverleaf, with ramps running north and south.

But the city of Cleveland refused to surrender part of the Burke Lakefront Airport property, insisting it would be used someday for runway expansion. Engineers therefore had to keep the Innerbelt south of the Shoreway and eliminate the cloverleaf. That resulted in a sharp curve and a hairpin ramp from Dead Man's Curve to Ohio 2 west.

Yet another accident at Dead Man's Curve—probably the only 90-degree turn in the U.S. Interstate system. *ODOT*

When the Innerbelt first opened in 1962, the speed limit was 50 mph, and the curve was not banked. Not surprisingly, trucks were overturning at an average of once a month, spilling everything from watermelons to newsprint across the road.

In 1965 the state installed warning signs and lowered the speed limit to 35 mph. But the accidents continued. In 1969 the state banked the curve, replaced the median guardrail with a concrete barrier, and cut rumble strips into the pavement. Police even asked trucking associations to mail warning letters to their members nationwide.

But the accidents continued.

The state has since improved lighting and added bigger signs, some with flashing lights.

And still the accidents continue.

A fix is coming

The good news is that Dead Man's Curve will eventually be fixed. It's part of a massive Innerbelt project that has been underway since 2011 and began with the replacement of the two original 1950s-era bridges over the Cuyahoga River.

"It is the daily recurring congestion and the crashes—that's what's driving us," said Dave Lastovka, Innerbelt Corridor manager for the Ohio Department of Transportation.

The northern end of the project, including Dead Man's Curve, is estimated to cost $400 million to $500 million and to begin sometime between 2027 and 2032, Lastovka said. Its enormous scope calls for:

- Relocating a sewer interceptor under I-90
- Replacing the CSX and Norfolk Southern railroad bridges over I-90
- Replacing the Superior, St. Clair, Hamilton, and Lakeside Avenues bridges over I-90
- Relocating the I-90 westbound ramp to Chester Avenue
- Realigning Dead Man's Curve north of Superior Avenue

All this will require taking some property east of the Innerbelt, including the Cleveland Mounted Police stables on East 38th Street.

When the work is finally done, Lastovka says, the curve will be safe to take at 60 mph. But no matter how safe it becomes, to Clevelanders it will always be Dead Man's Curve.

Why Is It Called
Whiskey Island?

Whiskey Island was never actually an island but a spit of land surrounded by marshes near the original mouth of the Cuyahoga River. Lorenzo Carter, Cleveland's first permanent White settler, built his farm there.

The current mouth of the Cuyahoga River was created by man, not by nature. When settlers first arrived, the river had a few more bends before it entered the lake. It curved westward along the shore and entered the lake at what is now West 54th Street. The land surrounding the river mouth was marshy and not well suited for development.

As commercial traffic on the river surged, particularly with the opening of the Ohio & Erie Canal, the city looked for ways to ease congestion while increasing river traffic. It decided to dig a new channel to the lake, one that would be—unlike the rest of the river—perfectly straight. That opened in 1827 and made navigation significantly easier—at least for that first (or last) half mile or so.

The original mouth of the river, after being cut off from the main river flow, eventually silted over. Later, this Old River Channel was reconnected to the river and dredged and widened to accommodate industry, including Great Lakes Towing Company and Great Lakes Shipyard, makers of the iconic red-and-green tugboats that serve throughout the Great Lakes.

After the new Cuyahoga shipping channel opened, the marshes dried up somewhat, making the land better suited for development. The Irish immigrants who dug the channel and worked on the docks settled in the area, which quickly gained a reputation as a rough-and-tumble slum. The Whiskey Island name came from a local distillery that served the hard-working, hard-drinking residents.

The Irish were displaced by the railroads in the 1850s, and Whiskey Island became almost exclusively industrial, home to ore docks, a salt mine, and the famous Hulett ore unloaders, which revolutionized cargo handling on freighters.

The salt mine is still there, but the docks and Huletts are long gone. By the 2010s, the area had become mostly recreational with marinas, volleyball courts, and bike trails. The art deco–styled former U.S. Coast Guard station at the tip of Wendy Park at the eastern end of Whiskey Island is its most prominent landmark.

Why Do So Many Suburbs Have "Heights" in Their Name?

Anyone planning a visit to eastern Cuyahoga County for the first time could be forgiven for expecting mountains. If not mountains, then at least lofty plateaus. After all, why else would so many suburbs have "Heights" in their names: Richmond Heights, Shaker Heights, Cleveland Heights, University Heights, Warrensville Heights . . .

In total, sixteen Cuyahoga County suburbs have "Heights" in their names, nearly all on the east side (Parma Heights, Broadview Heights, and Middleburg Heights are the exceptions).

Yet climbing Cedar Road or Mayfield Road east out of University Circle doesn't require crampons or pitons. The rise in elevation is, well, slight. A topographic map of the county shows that the eastern part is in general higher than the west, but the difference is only a few hundred feet.

In Northeast Ohio, "Heights" apparently has more to do with marketing than elevation. Adding it to the name of a town connotes an elevated status. And, in some cases, it was an easy way to distinguish a breakaway suburb from the mother community (see Parma and Parma Heights, Bedford and Bedford Heights).

The existing Heights suburbs were preceded by other attitudinally aspirational communities, such as the Euclid Heights and Ambler Heights developments in what is now Cleveland Heights. Shaker Heights and University Heights (originally Idlewood) both seceded from the village of Cleveland Heights but kept the suffix.

Interestingly, neighboring Geauga County, which has a higher overall elevation than Cuyahoga, doesn't have a single community with "Heights" in its name. Neither do Lake, Lorain, or Medina counties; Summit County has only Boston Heights.

How Can People Still Love the Browns Despite Decades of Crummy Football?

The Cleveland Browns test their fans.

Consider this:

The team moved to Baltimore in 1995, leaving the city without an NFL franchise for three seasons.

When a replacement team came to town in 1999 with the old name and colors, the new Browns set new records for futility. From their debut through the 2022 season, they had only three winning seasons, two playoff appearances, and one playoff win, and an abysmal overall record of 127-259. In 2017, the Browns were only the second team in NFL history to have an 0-16 season.

During that time, they had ten full-time head coaches, including two who were fired after a single season, and two interim coaches. One of the coaches, Hue Jackson, even accused them of trying to lose games to improve their draft position.

And they had had thirty-three starting quarterbacks, the most of any team over the same period.

Even going further back, the team's failings in big games earned their own shorthand among Cleveland sports fans: Red Right 88, The Drive, The Fumble.

As if the on-field disasters aren't bad enough, the team can be relied upon to regularly produce off-field drama, from an FBI investigation of the owner's truck stop business to the controversial 2022 signing of an alleged serial sex offender.

The worst franchise in town?

Now compare the Browns' record to that of the other pro sports franchises in town:

Rain or shine, bad season or worse season, fans pack the Muni Lot before any Browns game. *Erik Drost, via Flickr / CC BY 2.0*

The Indians/Guardians went to the World Series in 1995, 1997, and 2016. No victories, but at least they reached the championship. From 2012 to 2022, they made the playoffs six times, winning three series. They've had only nine losing seasons since 2000. Ownership has been stable, if stingy, and the team had just one manager—Terry Francona—from 2013 to 2023.

The two stretches when LeBron James was with the Cavs produced some of the most exciting moments in Cleveland sports history, including a championship in 2016 that ended the city's fifty-two-year title drought.

And yet, most of the chatter on sports talk radio is about the Browns. With the exception of the LeBron years and the great Indians teams of the 1990s, the Browns have dominated the sports landscape in Northeast Ohio. Fans dissect every move and speculate endlessly about what needs to be done to push the team over the top. Despite the ineptitude, the team continues to draw near sellout crowds and big TV audiences.

Even losing the team to Baltimore didn't cause fans to sour on the NFL. They even held a parade after the 0-16 season. Granted, it mocked the team's ineptitude, but it showed that the fans were still passionate and not apathetic, as might be expected.

And it's not as if everyone is clinging to past glories. Only middle-aged and older fans can remember the Kardiac Kids of 1980 or the teams from 1987 to 1990, when the Browns reached the AFC Championship Game three out of four years.

For longtime sportswriter Terry Pluto, the explanation lies in geography. Certain sports are simply more popular in different regions of the country. In Indiana, it's basketball. In Cincinnati, it's baseball. In the South, it's college football. And in Northeast Ohio and western Pennsylvania, it's pro football.

"This is football country. It just is," said Pluto, who jokes that you could draw 20,000 fans to watch a Browns helmet sitting on the 50-yard line of Cleveland Browns Stadium. And the NFL's relentless marketing of the draft, scouting combine, and training camps also makes it hard to avoid football, even during the offseason, he said.

Pluto, who has written books about all three Cleveland pro sports teams, said nothing is likely to permanently challenge the Browns' supremacy on the local sports scene.

"It runs in our DNA; it runs in our blood," he said.

Why Is Cleveland Still So Segregated?

Anyone who's lived here would not be surprised to learn that Greater Cleveland is one of the most segregated metro regions in the country.

According to the Brookings Institution, in 2018 Cleveland Metro was the fifth-worst region in the country for Black-White segregation. It's been segregated for so long that it's made its way into civic shorthand: Everyone living here understands that East Side means Black, while West Side means White (mostly ethnics).

And it's not just the core city that's segregated. Cuyahoga County generally reflects the same east-west divide, only the numbers are even more stark.

Nine Cuyahoga County suburbs have majority Black populations. All of them are on the East Side. By contrast, only four West Side suburbs have Black populations greater than 5 percent.

Racial segregation is not unique to Cleveland and Cuyahoga County, of course. Virtually every metro region in the country is segregated to a degree. But overall, segregation is gradually declining, according to the Urban Institute, a trend that Greater Cleveland stubbornly defies.

From integration to separation

Cleveland was not always as segregated as it is now. Until the end of the nineteenth century, the city was largely integrated with the small Black population well dispersed throughout the neighborhoods. Black and White children attended school together, and the races mixed at restaurants and in theaters.

That changed beginning in 1890, when increased migration

A problem that won't go away—racial imbalance in the population of Cleveland and its suburbs. *Cleveland Public Library*

from the South swelled Cleveland's Black population. By World War I, about 10,000 Black people lived in the city, concentrated in the Central Avenue district between the Cuyahoga River and East 40th Street, a neighborhood that also was home to immigrant Jews and Italians. Discrimination rose in response to the rising numbers as Black people were barred from an increasing number of commercial establishments.

Cleveland's Black population continued to grow during the Great Migration after World War I, overwhelming available housing. Black people were crammed into the overcrowded Woodland-Central area, which suffered from some of the highest rates of disease, poverty, and crime in the city.

Novelist Charles W. Chesnutt described the living conditions there: "The majority live in drab, middle or low class houses, none too well kept up . . . while the poor live in dilapidated, rack-rented shacks, sometimes a whole family in one or two rooms, as a rule paying higher rent than white tenants for the same space."

In response to those conditions, and out of the recognition that decent housing was partly the responsibility of government, the Cuyahoga Metropolitan Housing Authority was founded in 1933— the first such organization in the U.S. In 1937, CMHA built some of the nation's first public housing projects: Cedar-Central Apartments, Outhwaite Homes, and Lakeview Terrace (all of which still exist). More followed, the majority on the East Side.

The increased need for manufacturing labor during World War II drew more Black people to the city. When the Central neighborhood became too crowded, Black residents moved east and north, particularly into the Hough and Glenville neighborhoods, which had been vacated when Whites moved to large housing developments in suburbs such as Parma, Maple Heights, and Brooklyn.

Real estate agents hastened White flight through "blockbusting" while the banks' practice of redlining further contributed to segregated neighborhoods. The turnover was dramatic: Glenville was 67 percent Black in 1960 and 95 percent Black five years later. The city's Black population grew from 85,000 in 1940 to 251,000 in 1960.

The Housing Act of 1949, which created the urban renewal program, and the Federal Highway Act of 1956 did little to stop urban decay and, in many instances, accelerated it.

The Hough riots of 1966 and the Glenville Shootout of 1968 not only exposed the miserable conditions in Cleveland's ghettos but also further accelerated the White exodus. Court-ordered school busing, which began in 1979, convinced many of the remaining Whites to leave the district.

The Cuyahoga Plan of Ohio was one of several efforts to fight segregation. Formed in 1974 with foundation money, the private nonprofit established a housing information service and negotiated with lending institutions and real estate agents to end discriminatory practices.

Other forces at work

Racism and White flight aren't the only reasons for segregation. Historically, residents have moved away from the central city when they can afford to, said Thomas Bier, Ph.D., a senior fellow at Cleveland State University's Maxine Goodman Levin College of Urban Affairs and former director of the Center for Housing Research and Policy.

As the generally more affluent White residents moved out, Black people and other minorities moved into the neighborhoods they vacated, leaving behind, in turn, even worse housing. "The economically weak live in places that are rejected by those who have more income," Bier wrote in his 2017 book *Housing Dynamics in Northeast Ohio: Setting the Stage for Resurgence.*

Overbuilding housing in a region with a stagnant population also makes it easier for neighborhoods and communities to remain segregated.

The status quo

Segregation seems to have been accepted as an immutable reality in Cuyahoga County. Among residents' pressing concerns, it apparently ranks well below crime, the economy, and city services.

"We're as segregated as we were fifty years ago. It just seems so ingrained," said John Corlett, president and executive director of The Center for Community Solutions, an antipoverty organization.

Indeed, segregation in Cuyahoga County is getting worse. Euclid, South Euclid, and Richmond Heights saw the percentages of Black residents rise in the 2010s and 2020s as White residents moved out.

Only a few of Cleveland's suburbs are approximately racially balanced—Glenwillow, Richmond Heights, Bedford, South Euclid, Garfield Heights—and how long those communities can maintain that balance remains to be seen.

As the suburbs go, so follow the public schools.

A 2020 study by academician Beth Fry found that Cuyahoga public schools had segregation rates comparable to the 1960s, before court-ordered desegregation plans. The study found that East Side inner-ring suburbs had, on average, 78 percent Black enrollment, while their West Side counterparts had only 4 percent Black enrollment. White families in East Side suburbs are opting out of public schools in favor of parochial and private schools.

Hypersegregation

There is a term for Cleveland's extreme divide. Princeton sociologist Douglas Massey, who studied urban segregation in the 1980s, called it "hypersegregation." In one of his studies he found Cleveland to be among the most hypersegregated cities in the country.

"People growing up in such an environment have little direct experience with the culture, norms and behaviors of the rest of American society," Massey wrote, going on to explain the irony that in a diverse and densely populated society such as the United States, some individuals living in the inner city "are among the most isolated people on earth."

In a 2017 study, Massey revisited the data to see whether anything had changed. He found that Cincinnati and Columbus were no longer hypersegregated, but Cleveland still was.

"Although we've clearly made progress, the problems in many ways are becoming more intractable because there are now generations of black families in these places that have lived under conditions of hypersegregation and a high concentration of poverty," Massey said at the time.

10 Suburbs with Highest Black Population by Percentage

(Note: In 2020, the U.S. population was 12.4 percent Black; Ohio's population was 12.5 percent Black.)

Warrensville Heights (92%)   Oakwood (60%)
East Cleveland (90%)   Bedford (55%)
Highland Hills (83%)   Richmond Heights (52%)
North Randall (78%)
Bedford Heights (78%)
Maple Heights (74%)
Euclid (62%)

10 Suburbs with Highest White Population by Percentage

Bentleyville (97%)

Chagrin Falls (97%)

Valley View (96%)

Hunting Valley (95%)

Olmsted Falls (95%)

Independence (94%)

Bay Village (93%)

Cuyahoga Heights (93%)

Seven Hills (93%)

Mayfield Village (93%)

Do We Really Need All These Suburbs?

Cuyahoga County has 59 cities, villages, and townships, 13 municipal courts, and 11 school districts within its 1,246 square miles. Some people think that's too many.

Civic-minded reformers have argued for decades that the region would be better off with fewer local governments. They say merging cities would result in more efficient and affordable government for residents, lower taxes, and would save local jurisdictions from having to provide services they can no longer afford.

But it hasn't happened. The last local government in the county to disappear was Riveredge Township, a 48-acre strip of land north of Hopkins Airport that was divided and annexed by Cleveland and Fairview Park in 1992.

A Balkanized county

Compare Cuyahoga to Franklin County, home to Columbus. Franklin is roughly the same area as Cuyahoga with about 100,000 more people but with only forty-one cities, villages, and townships—eighteen fewer than Cuyahoga. Unlike Cleveland, Columbus aggressively pursued annexation of unincorporated neighboring communities as a requirement of access to city water.

Cleveland's failure to annex more of its neighbors during its early years of expansion resulted in a county that is a patchwork of local governments and communities, ranging in population from Cleveland's 376,000 to Linndale's 108. Eight communities have a population below 1,000; nineteen have fewer than 5,000 residents.

And almost every city and village has its own mayor, administrators, city council, police and fire departments, service department, and civic buildings. That's a lot of people doing the same jobs in different jurisdictions and a lot of identical fire engines sitting idle in identical stations on opposite sides of a city border.

Maintaining Cuyahoga County's fifty-nine cities can also lead to competition to provide amenities at taxpayer expense. Consider West Side neighbors Rocky River and Fairview Park. Each opened a multimillion-dollar recreation complex offering similar amenities, 1.5 miles apart, within a few years of each other.

Fairview Park's Gemini Center has proven to be a financial albatross. The city has struggled to make payments on the twenty-five-year bond issue that paid for the facility; in fact, it already refinanced them. Problems with the roof and HVAC systems have made it even more expensive. Would both cities have been better off if they'd collaborated on a single center?

Cities in the county also compete with each other for business, offering incentives and subsidies to get companies to relocate within their borders—a zero-sum game that does nothing to help the region and hurts the losing communities.

There are exceptions to this balkanization, of course. Regional authorities such as the Cleveland Metroparks, Northeast Ohio Regional Sewer District, Cuyahoga County Public Library, and Cleveland–Cuyahoga County Port Authority have shown that cooperation and regionalism can work.

East Cleveland

There is no better example of the resistance to civic consolidation than the long-discussed merger of Cleveland and East Cleveland.

To reformers, the merger makes so much sense that it simply has to happen. They consider East Cleveland, the poorest city in Ohio, a civic failure: poor, crime-ridden, and corrupt, with limited services, crumbling infrastructure, and a plunging population. It has lost nearly 40 percent of its residents since 2000, and its operating revenue has plummeted. It simply cannot afford to support its own police, fire, and service departments. Merging with Cleveland would give East Cleveland residents access to the services and resources of the larger, wealthier city.

In return, Cleveland would get a population bump of about 15,000 residents and potential redevelopment sites along Euclid Avenue. However, it also would have to take on East Cleveland's outstanding debts, the expense of bringing the city's infrastructure up to an acceptable standard, and the responsibility of providing services in a larger area.

Then there are the residents of East Cleveland, who, as down-trodden as their city is, have resisted its annexation despite the knowledge that their services almost certainly would improve. Under Ohio law, voters in both communities would have to approve a merger.

A merger proposal in 2016 died when East Cleveland City Council attached a list of demands that Cleveland officials judged unacceptable. The East Cleveland mayor who pushed for annex-ation was subsequently recalled, and merger talks have been dormant since.

If a city as desperate as East Cleveland can't agree to a merger with Cleveland, what chance is there that a comparatively better-off suburb like Brook Park or Warrensville Heights would do so?

City-county merger

While some advocates focus on merging a handful of neighbor-ing cities, others argue for a more sweeping approach, suggesting that Cleveland and the suburbs of Cuyahoga County follow the lead of cities like Indianapolis and Nashville and merge to form a single metropolitan government.

The resulting metro would have a population of about 1.3 million, which would make it the tenth-largest city in the U.S. The greater size would bring increased political clout, greater tax revenue, and access to millions more dollars in federal aid. But such a merger also would require overcoming an enormous number of barriers, and success would not be guaranteed. In 2019, a well-researched and well-funded proposal to merge St. Louis with its surrounding county failed before it even reached the ballot.

Over the decades, no organization has been a louder voice for civic consolidation than the Greater Cleveland League of Women Voters. It has been the driving force behind several such initiatives and has lobbied to change state law to make mergers easier. But its consolidation efforts have been futile.

"The public has always, these eighty-plus years, rejected giving up their local identities and autonomies, even if great economies can be shown to be gained," said Lynda Mayer, a former director of the LWV.

Another push is unlikely to happen anytime soon, she added.

"I think the effort would be futile, even if tantalizingly tempting to try. Those decisions must be made by new leaders and adopted by new generations of voters not as devoted to defending their local identities," she said.

Consolidating services

Consolidating government services is easier to accomplish than annexing whole cities; it allows cities to remain independent while sharing police and fire, emergency dispatch, health, purchasing, and other services. However, even that is not easily done.

The wealthy East Side communities of Moreland Hills, Orange, Pepper Pike, and Woodmere in 2013 completed a study of a possible merger but decided against it. However, the communities do share some services with neighboring communities. For example, Pepper Pike contracts emergency dispatch services from Beachwood and shares a building commissioner and building department employees with Moreland Hills.

In another example, in 2017 Cleveland and Cuyahoga County agreed that the county would take over city jail operations.

The financial impact of the COVID-19 pandemic on local government reignited discussion of sharing services, but it remains to be seen how much communities are willing to do.

Redrawing maps

Before becoming hemmed in by other communities, Cleveland grew into a city partly by absorbing its neighboring communities.

Many Cleveland neighborhoods were once independent settle-ments, including Glenville, South Brooklyn, Newburgh, West Park, and Collinwood. The most famous merger was with Ohio City, a rival that once skirmished with Cleveland over a bridge.

However, Cleveland eventually butted up against other cities, such as Lakewood and Parma, which rejected annexation. By the mid-1930s, Cleveland had stopped adding land and largely settled into its current boundaries.

Still, it's fun to print out a map of Cuyahoga County, start erasing municipal boundaries, and consolidate communities.

There are so many possibilities: Cuyahoga has three Olmsteds (North Olmsted, Olmsted Falls, and Olmsted Township)—does it really need more than one? Bratenahl is a wealthy lakefront enclave surrounded by Cleveland—should it be absorbed? What about the smaller suburbs to Cleveland's south, such as Linndale, Brooklyn, Brooklyn Heights, Newburgh Heights, and Cuyahoga Heights?

Should Parma and Parma Heights rejoin? What about Chagrin Falls and Chagrin Falls Township? There are a number of contig-uous suburbs that share school districts (Cleveland Heights and University Heights; Berea, Brook Park, and Middleburg Heights; South Euclid and Lyndhurst)—wouldn't it make sense for them to have a single city government as well as a school district?

It's unlikely that any of these will occur in the near future, but population loss and economic pressures might force it to happen someday.

Least Populous Cuyahoga County Communities

Linndale (108 residents)	Highland Hills (662)
Cuyahoga Heights (573)	Bentleyville (897)
Hunting Valley (627)	North Randall (954)
Woodmere (641)	Glenwillow (994)

Source: U.S. Census 2020

When Did Different Immigrants Arrive?

Cleveland has been shaped by waves of immigration, from the first settlers who followed Moses Cleaveland from Connecticut, to the Irish, Germans, Poles, and others who built the city in the late 1800s, to the Blacks who moved northward during the Great Migration in the twentieth century in search of jobs and to escape oppression.

More recently, the city has drawn Asian, Hispanic, and Middle Eastern immigrants.

In most cases, immigration has been influenced by outside factors, both domestic and international: the Potato Famine in Ireland, Eastern Europeans fleeing the Soviet Union, the Great Migration, the Cuban Revolution. People came to Cleveland for a variety of reasons, including jobs, safety, religious freedom, to escape persecution, and to join family.

Some groups, such as the Bavarian Jews, can trace to the year when their first member arrived. For others, the date of the first arrival is murkier. And, while immigration always has a start, it seldom reaches a definitive end.

Below is a rough guide to the greatest periods of immigration for various ethnic groups and nationalities:

Immigration Timeline

1796–1830—English (many from New England)

1830–70—German, Irish, English

1870–1914—Southern and Eastern European

1914–45—Southern Black, Mexican

1945–65—Puerto Rican, Appalachian, Ukrainian, Eastern European Jew

1965–Present—Middle Eastern, Asian, Southeast Asian, Chinese, Indian, Pakistani

How Did the Polish Boy Become Cleveland's Unofficial Official Sandwich?

Like the city in which it originated, the Polish Boy sandwich is a bit of a love-it-or-leave-it proposition.

A link of grilled or deep-fried kielbasa layered in fries and cole-slaw and slathered in sticky-sweet Kansas City–style barbecue sauce, all on a hot dog bun, the Polish Boy is Full Cleveland: ethnic, not particularly pretty, kinda messy, but ultimately satisfying.

The Polish Boy has been singled out by homeboy Michael Symon on The Food Network's *Best Thing I Ever Ate* and named one of the best sandwiches in America by *Esquire*, which called it "soul on white." The Daily Meal called it "one of the most insanely sloppy and delicious sandwiches in existence" and warned, "This is one serious sandwich; keep your Tums at the ready."

If the Polish Boy's four competing flavors aren't enough for you, there is the Polish Girl, which adds pulled pork to the combination. Some people will throw on cheese and whatever else might be handy, which is fine. After all, that's how the Polish Boy was created.

Who gets the credit for this signature sandwich?

As with many foods, its origins are hazy. However, Virgil Whitmore, who ran a restaurant in Cleveland's Mount Pleasant neighborhood starting in the 1940s, sometimes gets the nod. The story goes that he invented the Polish Boy by adding various ingredients he had around the kitchen to a smoked sausage. Other Whitmore's restaurant locations followed and helped make the Polish Boy popular. Only one Whitmore's Bar-B-Q remains open, in Warrensville Heights. It offers four variations on the classic Polish Boy.

A Polish Boy delivery vehicle. *Jim Sweeney*

Where else can you enjoy a Polish Boy? Several downtown hot dog carts sell them, but this is a sandwich that really requires a Formica-topped table with a fully stocked napkin dispenser. Here are a few spots you might want to try:

Banter, Shaker Heights

Gillespie's Map Room, Cleveland

Hot Sauce Williams, Cleveland

Seti's Polish Boys, Cleveland (food truck)

Kim's Wings, Cleveland and Euclid

Mabel's BBQ, Cleveland

Steve's Diner, Cleveland

Whitmore's Bar-B-Q, Warrensville Heights

Why Doesn't Cleveland Have More Downtown Retail?

You can do many things in downtown Cleveland. You can bowl; you can work out; you can get your hair cut; and you can eat and drink and watch professional sports.

What you can't do is shop at a department store. Downtown has retail, of course, but it's small and specialized, like Mike the Hatter, or utilitarian, like drugstores. There is a distinct shortage of the type of general retail that was once synonymous with downtown.

It hasn't always been that way. The stretch of Euclid Avenue between Public Square and East 13th Street once had so many upscale department stores that it was compared to New York's Fifth Avenue.

But as the suburbs grew in the 1950s, department stores opened branches closer to their customers, anchoring new malls like Parmatown, Euclid Square, and Severance Center. Eventually, the department stores closed their downtown flagships in favor of the bigger, newer suburban stores.

Downtown's decline in the 1960s and 1970s gave commuters little reason to stick around and shop after work. The collapse of downtown retail wasn't unique to Cleveland, of course. Cities all over the country, particularly in the Midwest, saw their cores empty out during this period.

Failed retail

There have been attempts to bring large-scale retail back to downtown, but they've largely failed.

The first was the The Galleria at Erieview, which opened in 1987 on the site of a plaza adjacent to the Erieview Tower at the corner of East 9th Street and St. Clair Avenue. It was the idea of developers

Richard and David Jacobs, who bought the tower (and also happened to own the Cleveland Indians).

The two-story, glass-enclosed center encompassing 207,000 square feet was part of downtown's initial resurgence and attracted national retailers such as Banana Republic and Sunglass Hut, but it struggled to keep tenants. It's changed ownership several times, and the main tenant in 2023 was the YMCA.

The second and grander attempt was Tower City Center. The former Union Terminal beneath Terminal Tower was gutted and rebuilt as a three-story, 367,000-square-foot shopping mall with an elaborate fountain the middle, an expansive food court, and retailers that had never been seen in Northeast Ohio before, like Fendi, Gucci, Versace, and Brooks Brothers.

And it worked—for a while. For the first time in decades, suburbanites traveled downtown to shop and see movies at Tower City Cinema. But gradually the appeal faded. Dillard's closed in 2002. (It was eventually replaced by a casino.) The upscale retailers left and were replaced by middle-market stores. When those departed, their spaces were left empty or replaced by low-rent stores more commonly found in strip malls. Tower City Cinemas closed in 2020. The once lively fountain has been shut off. Management has experimented with pop-up stores and locally owned shops.

The Tower City property was purchased in 2021 by Dan Gilbert's Bedrock. The billionaire businessman and Cavs owner has promised to revitalize the space.

The fact is that the era of the downtown mall is over—not just in Cleveland, but in every midsized city, said Michael Deemer, president and CEO of Downtown Cleveland. For example, City Center in Columbus opened in 1989 and closed in 2009. The space is now a park.

An unknown future

Downtown retail was building momentum before the COVID-19 pandemic hit in March 2020, Deemer said. The downtown population had reached 20,000, a figure Deemer called a critical mass of customers. The stretch of Euclid between Public and Playhouse squares, once home to so many department stores, was being remade by the construction of new residential buildings and the conversion of former office space. Many of those buildings were designed to feature storefront retail.

The pandemic devastated retail everywhere. Commuters worked from home, and downtown residents stayed in. Everyone learned to shop online. One retailer after another went out of business.

Recovery has been gradual. While the downtown population has continued to grow and is on target to reach 30,000 by 2030, only about 60 percent of former downtown workers are back in the city on any given weekday, Deemer said.

Retailers are reluctant to locate downtown without being certain of customer volume—and residents matter more than commuters, Deemer said, adding that he is confident that Cleveland will again be a retail hub.

While there probably will never again be anything as grand as the old downtown department stores or Tower City, that gap can be filled by smaller stores scattered throughout downtown, he said.

Former Downtown Department Stores

Bailey's (Ontario St. and Prospect Ave.)
F. W. Woolworth Co. (Euclid Ave. and E. 4th St.)
Halle Bros. (Playhouse Square)
May Co. (Euclid Ave. at Public Square)
The Higbee Co./Dillard's (Public Square)
Newman-Stearns (E. 12th St. and Walnut Ave.)
S. S. Kresge Co. (Euclid Ave. and E. 4th St.)
Sterling-Lindner-Davis (Euclid Ave. and E. 13th St.)
Taylor's (Euclid Ave. and E. 6th St.)

Why Did Millionaires' Row Disappear?

Drive along Euclid Avenue between Playhouse Square (starting around East 13th Street) and the East 80s, and it's hard to imagine this was once one of the grandest residential streets in the world.

But it's true: From 1870 to 1930, Euclid Avenue was home to some of the wealthiest and most powerful people in the country, including John D. Rockefeller, Secretary of State John Hay, Senator Marcus Hanna, and inventor Charles Brush. They competed to see who could build the grandest, most luxurious homes and employ the most servants to manage them. They hosted national and international political leaders, including presidents and ambassadors, and cultural icons. Mark Twain called Euclid "one of the finest streets in America."

Mere fragments of that splendor now remain, the mansions having long ago fallen victim to the growth of the city their residents built.

An escape from downtown

The industrialists first moved east along Euclid Avenue to get away from the downtown core where most made their fortune. The street offered a respite from the dirt and noise of the city center yet was still close enough for the magnates to take carriages to visit their mills and factories.

At its peak, from 1870 until 1920, Millionaires' Row was home to more than forty mansions. The first of these was built in the 1830s between Public Square and East 9th Street, a stretch of road that had been used as an informal raceway. Mansions on the north side of the street were generally bigger and more lavish, with larger estates and views of Lake Erie.

Ironically, it was the economic growth largely fueled by the Millionaires' Row industrialists that would eventually destroy the avenue. Not long after the first mansions were built, businesses began expanding eastward from downtown along Euclid, displacing some of the earliest Row manors and bringing noise, dust, and common folk uncomfortably close to the rich. The commerce the millionaires had created was now invading the retreat they'd built to escape it.

The millionaires fought back, using their power to persuade the city in 1896 to ban further commercial development between East 14th and East 105th Streets. Cleveland even rerouted streetcars between East 22nd and East 40th Streets so as not to disturb the denizens of the grand boulevard.

Not surprisingly, all this fueled a backlash. Critics decried the disparities between Millionaires' Row and nearby slums, many of whose residents worked in the factories owned by the Euclid Avenue barons. In 1915, the wealthy Row residents lost a legal battle that went all the way to the Ohio Supreme Court, and streetcar tracks were laid along Euclid Avenue.

The millionaires and their descendants fled, generally further east to Cleveland Heights and Shaker Heights and beyond, leaving behind their great houses. Some of the mansions fell to the wrecking ball to make room for car dealerships while others were converted to apartments. Others stood empty for years or housed a succession of tenants, who did little to preserve the grand homes.

The expanding city gave little consideration to the historic nature of the mansions and the value in their preservation until it was too late for most of them.

Remnants of the Row

Only four of the original Millionaires' Row mansions still stand, though none are used as residences. They are, from west to east:

After wealthy residents fled Euclid Avenue and Millionaires' Row, the wrecking ball came for their houses.

Mather Mansion, 2605 Euclid Avenue

The Mather Mansion, the last and largest house built on Millionaires' Row, was at the time the most expensive residence in the city. Its forty-five rooms included squash courts and a third-floor ballroom with space for three hundred guests. It had an eight-car garage and a 2.5-acre formal garden behind it.

Its original owner, Samuel Mather, was chairman of Pickands, Mather & Co., one of the largest shippers of iron ore in the country, and owned controlling interests in other transportation, banking, and manufacturing businesses. (The Steamship William G. Mather Museum, a retired iron ore freighter docked at the end of East 9th Street, is named after Samuel's half-brother.)

When the mansion was built in 1910, the city's commercial core already had begun to expand eastward, bringing with it the noise and congestion the millionaires had sought to avoid.

Located close to downtown at the western end of Millionaires' Row, the Mather Mansion would eventually be in danger of being demolished to make way for parking lots and commercial businesses.

When Mather died in 1931, the property transferred to the Cleveland Institute of Music, then to the Cleveland Automobile Club in 1940. In the mid-1950s, the houses between the mansion and East 30th Street were demolished to make way for I-90 and the Innerbelt, isolating the house even further.

Fortunately, Cleveland State University, which had acquired and demolished other Millionaires' Row homes to accommodate its expansion, decided to renovate this one. In 1973 it became one of the first Cleveland buildings to be listed on the National Register of Historic Places.

At one point, the university considered turning the Mather Mansion into a boutique hotel. It's now home to the Center for International Services and Programs. A CSU parking garage stands where the Mather garden once flourished.

The Stager Beckwith Mansion, 3813 Euclid Avenue

As one of the first grand houses to be built on Millionaires' Row, it's only fitting that the Stager Beckwith Mansion be one of the last standing.

It was constructed in 1866 by Anson Stager, general superintendent of Western Union Telegraph, but he lived in the house for only two years before selling it to Thomas Sterling Beckwith, the founder of one of Cleveland's first furniture and carpet stores, Beckwith, Sterling & Company.

When Beckwith's widow died in 1876, the house was sold to a neighbor, arc light inventor Charles Brush, who wanted control over who might move in next door. In 1913 Brush sold it to the University Club, an exclusive social organization. The University Club made extensive renovations and expansions to the house, growing it beyond its original 10,000 square feet. The University Club occupied the mansion until 2003 when it was sold to Myers University, which held it until 2007.

Empty and in foreclosure, it was bought for $50,000 in 2014 by a couple who donated it to the Children's Museum, which was relocating from its original University Circle site. The museum has since extensively renovated the building.

The Drury, 8625 Euclid Avenue

John D. Rockefeller not only became the richest man in the world; he made fortunes for others as well. That was the case with Francis Drury, who got rich selling kerosene stoves and heaters in collaboration with Rockefeller, who knew the stoves would help create a residential market for the kerosene that Standard Oil refined.

Like other later residents, Drury built his mansion toward the eastern end of the Row. Completed in 1910, the English Renaissance Tudor mansion had thirty-four rooms and totaled 25,000 square feet.

Later, Drury built a larger facsimile of the Euclid Avenue house on 155 acres in the far eastern suburb of Gates Mills and moved there in 1924. That house is now part of Gilmour Academy.

Drury donated his Euclid Avenue garden property, located across the street from the original mansion, to the fledgling Cleveland Play House, which eventually built its theater complex on the land. The Play House named one of its theaters the Francis Drury in his honor.

The house also had a fascinating history. In 1926, it was bought by the acting president of the Cleveland Museum of Art. His family then sold it to the Drury Club, an exclusive social club. From 1946 to 1972 it was the Florence Crittenton House, a maternity hospital and home for unwed mothers. It later became a treatment center for wayward parolees.

Eventually, in 1988, it was bought by The Cleveland Clinic Foundation, which renamed it the Foundation House. It's now largely used for receptions and ceremonies.

H.W. White Mansion, 8937 Euclid Avenue

The H.W. White Mansion, a 16,000-square-foot Victorian Gothic residence built between 1898 and 1901, was one of the last mansions to be built on Millionaires' Row.

The original owner was Henry Windsor White, the treasurer

of the White Sewing Machine Company, which later became the White Manufacturing Company.

After White's death in 1923, it was converted to apartments. A forty-three-year run as a funeral home followed. The International Center for Artificial Organs and Transplantation then owned it, followed by the Cleveland Health Museum, which used it for administrative offices until the museum closed in 2007. The Cleveland Clinic now uses it as a center for alumni affairs.

Legacy

Though Millionaires' Row is long gone, its legacy can still be felt throughout the region. Its former residents, elitists though they might have been, were largely or partly responsible for many of the finer things about Cleveland, including the Cleveland Orchestra and Severance Hall, Western Reserve Historical Society, Cleveland Play House, Cleveland Museum of Art, Museum of Natural History, Institute of Art, and the colleges that eventually formed Case Western Reserve University. Countless charities, including Hiram House, the YMCA, the YWCA, and Alta House, benefited from their largesse.

Euclid Avenue might never again be as grand as it was when the millionaires' carriages rolled down the boulevard, but those who know where to look can still find the remnants of its glorious past.

Tremont Has All Those Academic Street Names . . . But Where's the College?

A neighborhood with streets named Professor, Literary, University, and College ought to be home to an institution of higher learning.

But while Tremont, the neighborhood in question located on Cleveland's near West Side, has plenty of bars and restaurants, it doesn't have a college or university anywhere near it. So why the academic street names?

Because Tremont was once home to Cleveland University, the city's first institute of higher learning. But the school didn't last long enough to hand out a single four-year degree.

Cleveland University was chartered by the Ohio General Assembly in 1851. Its first president was Asa Mahan, who had recently resigned as head of Oberlin Institute, the precursor to Oberlin College. A number of students followed Mahan from Oberlin to the new school.

The first classes were held in a building on Ontario Avenue downtown, but university trustees had their eyes on a 275-acre site across the river in the area now known as Tremont. Streets were laid out and named appropriately, and a three-story building was erected.

President Mahan and the trustees dreamed big. Not only did they envision a university of national renown but also an orphan asylum, a nursing home, and a female seminary on the same site. Their plan was to name the community University Heights. (That name would later be taken by the East Side suburb that is home to John Carroll University.)

Jim Sweeney

Cleveland University started well. The college awarded eight degrees in June 1852 but quickly fell on hard times. Mahan resigned at the end of the year. One of the school's main benefactors died that winter. And at the end of the following academic year, Cleveland University was liquidated.

A private secondary school opened on the site, and Cleveland University faded from memory. Except for the street names. The city of Cleveland eventually became home to two universities (neither connected to the Tremont institution): Cleveland State University and Case Western Reserve University.

What Are the Cultural Gardens?

To drivers zipping along Martin Luther King Boulevard between University Circle and the lakefront, the Cleveland Cultural Gardens flash by in a blur of stone and statues.

The thirty-five gardens along MLK and East Boulevard in Rockefeller Park are best experienced on foot and a few at a time. In total, they provide a textured picture of the many ethnic groups that formed the city and continue to shape it.

Rockefeller Park was created in 1896 as part of the celebration of Cleveland's centennial on land donated by oil magnate John D. Rockefeller. The Cultural Gardens were started in 1916 with the first installation, the Shakespeare Garden, brainchild of Leo Weidenthal, an Anglophile and publisher of the *Jewish Independent* newspaper. He and Charles Wolfram formed the Cleveland Cultural Gardens Federation to bring about a chain of gardens, which now stretches from University Circle to the Shoreway.

Each garden is planned, developed, and sponsored by the community it celebrates. In many cases, the design is the work of local architects and artists who come from the community being honored. Not surprisingly, the oldest gardens reflect the city's earliest immigrant groups, primarily European, but in recent decades the Gardens have become more diverse with additions from the Middle East and Asia. Another ten to twelve gardens are in various stages of planning, said Dan Hanson, a Federation board member and tireless booster of the Gardens.

In addition to being a collage of the different ethnic groups and nationalities that comprise Cleveland, the Cultural Gardens are an education in various cultures with tributes to artists, heroes, poets, and politicians often unknown to those outside their community.

For example, the Czech Cultural Garden features statues of Jan

Amos Komensky, considered the father of modern education, and T. G. Masaryk, president of Czechoslovakia, while the African American Garden educates visitors on the Middle Passage.

The annual One World Day and Parade of Flags celebration draws tens of thousands of people to the Gardens, which sprawl over more than 250 acres. They have been visited by nine heads of state.

"The presidents and prime ministers can't believe there is a tribute to their nations right here in Cleveland, Ohio. They're deeply moved," Hanson said.

The Cultural Gardens can also reflect what's happening in the real world, he said. For example, when Yugoslavia broke up in 1992, the Yugoslavian Cultural Garden was dissolved soon after. That site is now home to the Slovenian Garden, while the Serbian and Croatian communities created their own monuments.

And when one community adds a bust or feature to its garden, its rivals and neighbors are often moved to do the same. Sort of like a statuary arms race.

List of Cultural Gardens

African American	Ethiopian	Latvian	Russian
Albanian	Finnish	Lebanese	Scottish
American	German	Lithuanian	Serbian
Armenian	Greek	Mexican	Slovakian
Azerbaijani	Hebrew	Pakistani	Slovenian
British	Hungarian	Peace Gardens of	Syrian
Chinese	Indian	the Nation	Turkish
Croatian	Irish	Polish	Ukrainian
Czech	Italian	Romanian	Uzbek
Estonian	Korean	Rusin	Vietnamese

Why Do Browns Fans Hate the Steelers So Much?

It was the aftermath of a Browns-Steelers game at Municipal Stadium in the late 1980s. The Browns had lost, and a crowd of sullen fans was milling about in the Municipal Parking Lot. Several charter buses filled with Pittsburgh fans idled nearby in bumper-to-bumper eastbound traffic on the Shoreway.

Taunts were exchanged. Obscene gestures followed. Bottles were thrown. And then the doors opened, and Steelers fans poured out of the idling buses and into the parking lot to brawl with Browns fans, a fight that raged until traffic began moving again and the Pittsburgh fans retreated to their buses.

It was just one incident among many, but it captures well the mutual loathing, the violence, and the passion that makes the Browns-Steelers rivalry one of the fiercest in sports.

But why is this rivalry so much more intense than the ones between the Browns and other teams, like the Baltimore Ravens, which used to be the Browns, or the Cincinnati Bengals, which were founded and once led by the greatest coach in Browns history?

Too close for comfort

It's said that familiarity breeds contempt, and Cleveland and Pittsburgh have more in common than either city likes to admit. To start, they're only 134 miles apart by the Ohio and Pennsylvania Turnpikes, which makes it easy for fans to travel to away games.

And the cities have similar backgrounds. Both blue-collar towns and industrial powerhouses that crashed hard in the 1970s and 1980s, they struggled to find their place in the New Economy (though Pittsburgh has done a better job of it). Cleveland has a Great Lake, and Pittsburgh has three rivers.

The familiarity extends to the field as well. It's not lost on Browns fans that former Steelers quarterback and future Hall of Famer Ben Roethlisberger is from Ohio (Lima), played college ball in Ohio (Miami), and was passed over by the Browns in the 2004 draft.

Former Steelers head coach Bill Cowher played and coached for the Browns before joining Pittsburgh. Another legendary Steelers coach, Chuck Noll, was born in Cleveland and played for the Browns. Steelers linebacker James Harrison, who terrorized the Browns for years, was born in Akron and played for Kent State, which also was the alma mater of Jack Lambert. And Marty Schottenheimer played for the Steelers before becoming the Browns' head coach.

Big hits and big games

The two teams first played in 1950, in what was the Browns' first game in the NFL after moving over from the All-America Football Conference. Over the next two decades, Cleveland dominated the rivalry. The tide turned in the 1970s when Pittsburgh's great "Steel Curtain" teams won four Super Bowls from 1975 to 1980. The Steelers have largely had the upper hand since and hold an overall series lead. At times, it has seemed less of a rivalry and more of a mismatch.

Like any great rivalry, this one has had its share of memorable games and moments.

In October 1976, Browns defensive end Joe "Turkey" Jones upended Steelers QB Terry Bradshaw and planted him headfirst into the turf at Municipal Stadium, knocking him out of the game. This is still regarded as one of the most ferocious sacks in NFL history.

The Browns' first game "back" as an expansion franchise in 1999 was against the Steelers, who pounded them 43-0. Later that season, the Browns upset their rivals in Pittsburgh.

In 2011, Steelers linebacker James Harrison knocked Browns quarterback Colt McCoy out of the game with a vicious hit that resulted in a one-game suspension.

In November 2019, Browns defensive end Myles Garrett clubbed Steelers quarterback Mason Rudolph with his own helmet.

In January 2021. the Browns beat the Steelers to earn their first playoff win in twenty-six years.

Every win, every loss, every sack and TD celebration resonates that much more because it's Browns versus Steelers.

Envy

Though Browns fans would be loath to admit it, there is an element of envy to the rivalry. While the Browns have flailed and foundered, the Steelers since the 1970s have been the model of a successful small-market franchise: stable ownership, stable management, stable coaching, and stable quarterbacking.

Consider: From the Browns' return in 1999 through the 2022 season, the Steelers had fourteen starting quarterbacks with the overwhelming number of games played by a single QB, Ben Roethlisberger. The Browns had thirty-four.

The Steelers had two head coaches in that period, compared to the Browns' twelve, and one owner, the Rooney family, while the Browns shuffled from Al Lerner to his son, Randy Lerner, to the Haslams.

Worst of all, at least for Browns fans, the Steelers had only two losing seasons from 1999 to 2022, compared to the Browns' nineteen.

Behind enemy lines

Perhaps no Browns fan is more intimate with the rivalry than Dr. Paul Carson, head of the Pittsburgh chapter of the Browns Backers Worldwide club. Carson grew up in Cleveland Heights and Solon before studying medicine at the University of Pittsburgh. There he met and married his wife and found himself living in the heart of enemy territory.

Despite having lived in Pittsburgh for more years than Cleveland, Carson's loathing of the Steelers has not waned.

"I can root for every other team in Pittsburgh. I'm a Pirates fan, I'm a Penguins fan, but I can't be a Steelers fan," he said.

He revived the local Browns Backers chapter when the team returned to the NFL in 1999, and for every game approximately one hundred fans—almost all of them transplanted Clevelanders—congregate at a local bar to cheer for the Browns. It hasn't always been easy to find a place willing to host the club, Carson said, adding that this is the sixth or seventh establishment over the past few decades.

Except on game days and when surrounded by friends, being a Browns fan in Steel City requires a certain amount of discretion. "You can't show anything," Carson said. "You can't put a sticker on your car or have a Browns license plate holder because someone will mess with your car."

Despite all of that, Carson said he will never let the rivalry go: "It's in our blood."

Whatever the future holds for the two teams, their twice-a-year contests will continue to hold a special, heated place in the hearts of Browns fans.

How Did Cleveland's Jewish Community Become Centered in the East Side Suburbs?

It was common in the nineteenth century for ethnic groups emigrating to Cleveland to settle in the same neighborhoods. Living in a tight-knit community made life easier for newcomers; their neighbors shared the same faith and customs, spoke the same language, wore the same clothes, and ate the same food.

Over time, as immigrants acclimated to their new homes and reared native-born children, once tight-knit neighborhoods tended to disperse. Greater affluence meant immigrants and their children could afford homes in nicer neighborhoods, and learning English made it easier to live anywhere in the city.

While there are still city neighborhoods that are strongly identified with specific ethnicities—Slavic Village, AsiaTown, Ohio City, Little Italy—the people of those nationalities have largely dispersed throughout Cuyahoga County and Northeast Ohio. For example, the Irish and the Germans, two of the most populous groups, are scattered throughout the region without easily identifiable centers.

Jews are an exception, however. While the community has been mobile and is more dispersed than it used to be, it has remained more geographically concentrated than most other immigrant groups.

The overwhelming majority of Jews live in a handful of eastern Cuyahoga County suburbs. Need proof? There are thirty-eight Jewish congregations in the county; thirty-seven of them are on the East Side.

According to a 2011 study from the Jewish Federation of Cleveland, approximately 27 percent of the Jewish population at that time lived in the older, inner-ring suburbs of Shaker Heights, Cleveland Heights, and University Heights, collectively known as The Heights. But the city in Northeast Ohio with the largest Jewish population is Beachwood, which is roughly 90 percent Jewish.

Not surprisingly, most of the region's temples and Jewish community centers are on the East Side as well.

Moving eastward

As with most ethnic groups that first came to Greater Cleveland long ago, the Jewish community got its start downtown and gradually spread outward in search of a better life.

A group of fifteen Jews from Unsleben, Bavaria, arrived in Cleveland in 1839, encouraged by fur trader Simson Thorman, an Unsleben native who had settled in the city and recruited his former townspeople to join him.

They settled originally in the Central Market area southeast of Public Square and then, as the population grew, moved to the Woodland neighborhood around East 55th Street. The original group of Bavarian Jews was augmented in the following decades by the arrival of Orthodox Jews from Hungary, Poland, Romania, Russia, and elsewhere. Despite substantial differences between the groups, they tended to live near each other, said Sean Martin, associate curator of Jewish history at the Western Reserve Historical Society.

In the early twentieth century, as the Jewish community reached a peak of about 87,000, the center shifted eastward again to the neighborhoods of Kinsman, Glenville, and Hough. East 105th Street became so crowded with Jewish businesses that it was referred to as the "Yiddeshe Downtown."

In the 1930s and 1940s, Jewish households began to leave those neighborhoods for the more affluent and spacious Heights communities. Fleeing overcrowding, noise, and pollution, they were also moving away from Black residents who had begun moving into the neighborhoods, Martin said.

Why didn't they move west?

"Believe it or not, the (Cuyahoga) River is a real barrier, at least psychologically," Martin said.

Another reason for the cohesiveness, he said, is that the Jewish community, more than most, is centered around its institutions—congregations, schools, and social service organizations—which remained on the East Side. For example, because Orthodox Jews walk to temple during Shabbat, they must live nearby. The Jewish Federation of Cleveland, the umbrella organization for Northeast Ohio Jewish groups, also has done a good job of keeping the community intact, Martin said.

In the 1960s, the Jewish community continued to push eastward into Beachwood, South Euclid, Solon, Pepper Pike, Moreland Hills, and Orange. Not surprisingly, Jewish temples, congregations, schools, and community organizations followed the population. In some cases, Jews moving into these new cities had to overcome restrictive property covenants put in place to keep them out.

While parts of the Heights still have a distinctively Jewish flavor, particularly along Taylor Road and parts of Cedar Road, the hub of the Jewish community has been Beachwood for at least the past two decades. Ironically, that was one of the suburbs that once tried to keep Jews out.

Beachwood is now home to the *Cleveland Jewish News*, the Jewish Federation of Cleveland, the Mandel Jewish Community Center, the Maltz Museum of Jewish Heritage, Menorah Park, and multiple congregations.

Will Beachwood remain the center of the Jewish community? If history is any indicator, Jews will continue to move eastward; indeed, more have been moving to Solon and Twinsburg, but it is unlikely that Beachwood will be replaced as the Jewish hub anytime soon.

Why Were the Indians Renamed the Guardians?

At the end of the 2021 baseball season the Cleveland Indians ended their 106-year existence. The script Indians sign on the Progressive Field scoreboard was dismantled and lowered by crane.

Major league baseball didn't leave town, of course, and the team's roster the following season bore a strong resemblance to the previous year's squad, but the Cleveland Indians had been replaced by the Cleveland Guardians.

Why, after so long, did the team change its name? And why, despite all the ferocious animals, mythological figures, and other names it could have chosen, did it pick the Guardians?

How the Indians got their name

Though the name "Indians" lasted the longest, Cleveland's professional baseball teams had other names before it, including the Blues, Forest Citys, and Bronchos. To understand the history of the nomenclature, it helps to know that team names weren't always that big of a deal.

In the early days of baseball, team names weren't chosen through fan surveys or as a result of exhaustive marketing research. They weren't selected with an eye toward merchandising, logos, appeal to various demographics, or judged as a possible offense to any racial, ethnic, or religious groups. Some teams didn't have formal names (or had several at the same time) but were simply referred to by their home cities. Teams regularly changed names, sometimes even swapping names with other teams.

Perhaps most remarkable is how often the names were chosen

by sportswriters rather than the teams themselves. A columnist or reporter would refer to a team by a nickname; if the fans liked it, it caught on. Sportswriters were at least partly responsible for the names of the Cardinals, Pirates, Braves, Cubs, Dodgers, Yankees, and, yes, Indians.

In those early days of the sport, long before free agency, a team could even be named after a player. That was the case in Cleveland from 1903 to 1914, when the team was named the Naps in honor of Hall of Fame player-manager Napoleon Lajoie. When Lajoie left after the 1914 season, the team needed a new name.

Team owners asked sportswriters to come up with one, and they chose the Indians, possibly because the Boston Braves had won the World Series the year before.

Some people have said the team was named in honor of former player Louis Sockalexis, the first Native American to play major league baseball. That seems unlikely, however. Though Sockalexis was a star with the Cleveland Spiders for several years, he was dismissed from that club in 1899 due to his alcoholism and died in 1913. His popularity was never such that the team would have been named after him.

The rise and fall of Chief Wahoo

The Indians name was predeceased by the team's longstanding logo and mascot, Chief Wahoo. The red-skinned, hook-nosed logo (one of at least three variations over the years) was finally retired after years of growing objections to the use of Native American imagery in professional sports and Wahoo in particular.

An early cartoon version of Chief Wahoo called "The Little Indian" was created in 1932 by a *Plain Dealer* cartoonist. The caricature was used on the front page to announce the results of the previous day's game. In 1947, owner Bill Veeck hired a design firm to create a logo for the team and approved a grinning, head-band-wearing figure drawn in the cartoon style of the times.

However, it took a while for him to be named. The Chief Wahoo moniker had been around for years before the logo; it had even been applied to a Native American player for the Indians, Allie Reynolds. The name did not become attached to the logo until 1952, when someone in a costume based on the logo appeared at a children's party on Public Square. Sportswriters subsequently began referring to the logo as Chief Wahoo, and it stuck.

In 1951 the mascot was redesigned with a smaller nose and red skin instead of an earlier, yellow, version, but it otherwise remained largely unchanged.

From 1962 through 1994, a twenty-eight-foot-tall, neon-lit sign of Chief Wahoo at bat hung over Gate D at Municipal Stadium. When the stadium was demolished, the sign was donated to the Western Reserve Historical Society, which refurbished it and added it to its collection.

Chief Wahoo, one of the most distinctive logos in sports, became a figure of controversy beginning in the 1960s as part of a bigger movement opposed to the use of Native American names and symbols by sports teams.

It became an Opening Day tradition for Native American activists and supporters to protest outside the ballpark, trading insults with fans who defended the logo, sometimes while wearing feathered headdresses and warpaint.

Without ever admitting that the logo was offensive, the team began distancing itself from Wahoo in the 2010s, shifting to the use of a block "C", which became the primary logo in 2013. Chief Wahoo was officially retired after the 2018 season, and MLB has banned its use on future Baseball Hall of Fame plaques.

Chief Wahoo is still embraced by some fans, who continue to defiantly wear the gear.

Why the Guardians?

Dropping the logo did not initially signal that the team would also change its name, but the path had been set. In 2020 it was announced that the Indians name was being dropped, and the process of finding a replacement began. The club said it started with a list of nearly 1,200 possibilities. Fan speculation centered

Guardians of Traffic tower above the Hope Memorial (Lorain-Carnegie) Bridge.
Erik Drost, via Flickr / CC BY 2.0

on the Spiders, Rockers, Buckeyes (a salute to Cleveland's Negro Leagues team), Blues, Blue Sox, and Municipals, among others.

Guardians was a surprising choice. But when fans took a little time to think about it, it made some sense. It's short for the Guardians of Traffic, four statues on the Hope Memorial Bridge (formerly the Lorain–Carnegie Bridge) near Progressive Field. The art deco–style statues, designed by sculptor Henry Hering and architect Frank Walker, were built in 1932. Each statue holds a different means of transportation in its hands: a hay wagon, covered wagon, stagecoach, an automobile, and four types of construction trucks. They represent the progress of transportation.

Even though they're holding trucks and wagons rather than something more heroic like a sword or torch, the Guardians are ridiculously photogenic and noble looking. However, although highly recognizable among residents, they had never been a symbol of the city the way the Gateway Arch is in St. Louis or the Space Needle is in Seattle.

What do the statues have to do with baseball? Nothing. Absolutely nothing. So why were they chosen as the new name? Team owner and CEO Paul Dolan put it this way in a letter to fans published on cleveland.com:

We wanted a name that strongly represents the pride, resiliency and loyalty of Clevelanders. "Guardians" reflects those attributes that define us while drawing on the iconic Guardians of Traffic just outside the ballpark on the Hope Memorial Bridge. It brings to life the pride Clevelanders take in our city and the way we fight together for all who choose to be part of the Cleveland baseball family. While "Indians" will always be a part of our history, our new name will help unify our fans and city as we are all Cleveland Guardians.

There was one snag, though. It turned out Cleveland already had a Guardians sports team: A men's roller derby squad had been competing under the name since 2017. The roller derby team sued but reached a settlement in 2021 that allows both teams to compete under the name "Guardians."

Reaction to the new name and accompanying logo has been mixed, with some fans vowing to continue to wear Indians and Chief Wahoo gear while others welcomed the change. Even former president Donald Trump weighed in, attacking the new name as an affront to fans and Native Americans. But with a successful 2022 season, an exciting young team, and an appearance in the playoffs, the Guardians quickly set about converting fans to the new name.

Cleveland Baseball Teams

Forest Citys (1871-72)

Blues (1879-84, 1887-88)

Spiders (1889-99)

Bronchos (1902)

Naps (1903-14)

Indians (1915-2021)

Guardians (2022-?)

One-time Baseball Team Names that Ought to Be Resurrected

Bridegrooms

Doves

Highlanders

Orphans

Perfectos

Superbas

Teams with Native American Names

Professional (Major League)

Atlanta Braves (MLB)
Chicago Blackhawks (NHL)
Kansas City Chiefs (NFL)
Golden State Warriors (NBA)

College

Florida State University Seminoles
University of Utah Utes
Central Michigan University Chippewas
San Diego State University Aztecs
Alcorn State University Braves

Teams that Changed Their Names

Professional

Cleveland Indians to Guardians (MLB)
Edmonton Eskimos to Elks (CFL)
Washington Redskins to Washington Commanders (NFL)

College

Miami (Ohio) University Redskins to RedHawks
Eastern Michigan University Hurons to Eagles
University of North Dakota Fighting Sioux to Fighting Hawks
Southeastern Oklahoma State University Savages to Savage Storm
St. John's University Redmen to Red Storm

Why Doesn't Cleveland Have an NHL Team?

Cleveland is surrounded by National Hockey League franchises in Buffalo, Pittsburgh, Detroit, Chicago, and Columbus, yet it doesn't have a team of its own. Cleveland and Milwaukee are, in fact, the only major Great Lakes cities that don't.

So why is that?

Here's a clue: What was the last franchise among the four major sports (baseball, football, basketball, and hockey) to fold?

Answer: The NHL Cleveland Barons.

Failure of a franchise

Cleveland had an NHL team, the Barons, from 1976 to 1978. In its two seasons, it was one of the worst teams in NHL history.

It was not a homegrown team but a relocated one. The California Golden Seals, one of six teams added by the NHL in 1967, was struggling. Cleveland seemed like a safe bet as its new home. After all, the city had a long history of supporting minor-league hockey; in fact, the Montreal Canadiens very nearly relocated to Cleveland in the 1930s.

Golden Seals owner Mel Swig even renamed the team the Barons to tap into Cleveland's affection for its former American Hockey League (AHL) franchise of the same name. Plus, the new team would play in the Richfield Coliseum, which opened in 1974 and would be the newest arena in the NHL.

But things didn't work out so well. The Barons went 47-87-26 over two seasons, finishing last in their division. They were also dead last in attendance at the Big House on the Prairie, as the Coliseum was known. Attendance was so bad that the team struggled

The AHL Cleveland Barons won the Calder Cup in 1953. The later NHL version of the Barons didn't fare so well. *Cleveland Public Library*

to make payroll. It only finished its final season because the NHL Players' Association took out a loan, and other team owners kicked in some money.

At the time, Defenseman Bob Stewart, the Barons' player representative, was quoted as saying: "We got to the point where we felt like no one cared—not the Players' Association, not the fans, not the club, not even the league. We'd even like to be booed, anything that shows someone's interested."

After the 1977–78 season, the team merged with the Minnesota North Stars. Cleveland was without a pro hockey team until the Lumberjacks of the International Hockey League took to the ice in 1992.

A hockey town

It's not that Cleveland doesn't support hockey. In the past century it's been home to eight different minor league franchises, in addition to the NHL Barons. The original minor league Barons, hugely successful in the 1940s and 1950s, were informally considered the seventh NHL franchise in addition to the original six teams. In 1942, the NHL even invited the Barons to join the league, but the team's owner declined for fear the move would destroy the AHL.

Cleveland's current team, the Monsters, is an AHL club and Columbus Blue Jackets affiliate that has played here since the 2007–8 season. It's been successful at the ticket office and on the ice, even winning the Calder Cup in 2016.

"It's a hidden gem in this town," said David Uhrin, a Monsters season ticket holder and treasurer of the Cleveland Hockey Booster Club.

The club, which was established in 1948 as the official booster organization of the original Barons, has endured even during those periods when Cleveland didn't have a hockey team, embracing every subsequent franchise.

Today, in addition to supporting the Monsters, the club promotes the game at all levels and even awards college scholarships.

According to Cleveland Monsters season ticket holder Len Matlock, most Cleveland fans are content to have a team in the AHL, the sport's top minor league. That's because tickets are more affordable and minor league status gives fans more access to players.

"We enjoy the team we have and what we can do with it," Matlock said.

Will Cleveland ever get another NHL team?

It's not likely. In addition to its failed NHL history, the Cleveland market might simply be too small to support a fourth major league franchise in addition to the Browns, Guardians, and Cavaliers. While the Browns are a steady sellout, the other two teams often struggle at the gate. A fourth major league club might simply spread the fan revenue base too thin.

The large number of NHL teams nearby might limit a Cleveland team's ability to draw fans from outside the market, though having three teams within three hours' drive does lend itself to establishing regional rivalries.

"If you think about where Cleveland is geographically, the NHL doesn't need us," Matlock said.

The most recent NHL expansion cities have been Seattle (2021), Las Vegas (2017), Columbus and Minneapolis–St. Paul (2000), and Nashville (1998). It's speculated that the next city to land a franchise is likely to be Quebec, Houston, Kansas City, Milwaukee or Hamilton, Ontario.

Cleveland Professional Hockey Teams

Cleveland Indians—1929-33, International Hockey League, Elysium Arena

Cleveland Falcons—1934-37, International Hockey League/International American Hockey League, Elysium Arena

Cleveland Barons—1937-72, American Hockey League, Cleveland Arena

Cleveland Knights—1949-50, Eastern Hockey League, Cleveland Arena

Cleveland Crusaders—1972-76, World Hockey Association, Cleveland Arena, 1972-74, Richfield Coliseum, 1975-76

Cleveland Barons—1976-78, National Hockey League, Richfield Coliseum

Cleveland Lumberjacks—1992-2001, International Hockey League, Richfield Coliseum, 1992-94, Gund Arena, 1995-2001

Cleveland Barons—2001-6, American Hockey League, Gund Arena

Lake Erie Monsters—2007-present, American Hockey League, Rocket Mortgage Field House

How Did Cleveland Become a Punchline?

Anyone who watched *The Tonight Show* in the 1970s got used to hearing host Johnny Carson joke about Cleveland: "What's the difference between Cleveland and the Titanic? Cleveland has a better orchestra!"

In the 1980s, comedian Yakov Smirnoff joked: "In the United States you make fun of Cleveland. In Russia we make fun of . . . Cleveland."

Even Bob Hope, whose family emigrated to Cleveland when he was a child, regularly made fun of his adopted hometown.

How exactly did Cleveland, which once billed itself as "The Greatest Location in the Nation," become known instead as "The Mistake on the Lake"?

It's not as if Cleveland was the only city to be the butt of jokes. Buffalo, Burbank, Detroit, Peoria, and a host of others, most in the Midwest, were also relegated to punchlines. But no other city was targeted as much as Cleveland.

Why?

Well, to be honest, there was a lot to make fun of. In the 1970s, Cleveland seemed to symbolize everything wrong with American cities, the Midwest, the Rust Belt, and even the whole country. It was poor, dirty, violent, and in decline. A number of incidents made the jokes too easy: the 1969 Cuyahoga River fire; Mayor Ralph Perk accidentally setting his hair on fire with a welding torch in 1972; the Ten-Cent Beer Night Riot at the stadium in 1974; the steady decline of the once-formidable Browns and the ongoing futility of the Indians; civic default in 1978; the antics of Boy Mayor Dennis Kucinich.

The man who turned the city into a joke

Northeast Ohio has a rich comedy history. Over the years, several talented performers and writers left Cleveland for Hollywood—including some who went on to write for Johnny Carson. But no one was more responsible for turning the city into a punchline than the late Jack Hanrahan, a transplanted Clevelander who wrote for everything from *Get Smart* to *The Sonny and Cher Comedy Hour.* It was as a writer for *Rowan & Martin's Laugh-In* that Hanrahan made his hometown the butt of joke after joke.

As Hanrahan recounted, the *Laugh-In* writers had been told by NBC executives to stop making Polish jokes and needed a new target. Hanrahan, who was born in West Park and attended the Cleveland Institute of Art and John Carroll University, suggested his hometown.

The jokes started and just kept coming:

In Cleveland, Velveeta cheese can be found in the gourmet section of the supermarket.

Attention Cleveland! Your river is on fire.

Definition of a luxurious Cleveland cocktail lounge: a bottle of Seagram's with a brown bag around it.

In Cleveland, the St. Patrick's Day parade consists of 50,000 Jewish onlookers watching the help walk by.

In a 2002 interview with *Cleveland Magazine*, Hanrahan explained why Cleveland was such fertile comic soil:

"Cleveland gives you the atmosphere for it," he said. "Every time I've written anything of real value, I've had to go back to that setting for most of it. I still feel more comfortable with family and friends there because there's no putting on an act; there's no bullshit. I've incorporated that into the story. And the neighborhood bars where I used to hang out.

"And it's so much easier writing from truth. The humor flows. You don't even have to make jokes up. It flows. It flows like water through the sewers of Cleveland."

In on the joke

Clevelanders sometimes joined in the fun. Two of the most popular T-shirt slogans in the 1970s were "Cleveland: You Gotta Be Tough" and "Cleveland: Default's Not Mine." But in the 1980s, as Cleveland billed itself as "The Comeback City," residents developed a thin skin. Their thinking was that it was OK for Clevelanders to make fun of the city but not for outsiders to do so. Radio station WMMS, for example, reacted to any slight of the city by urging listeners to flood the offending TV network or out-of-town radio station with angry calls.

Luckily, that sort of defensive provincialism has largely died down. Clevelanders feel secure enough to take the occasional jab in stride. Even the "burning river" joke has been co-opted and applied to a local craft beer and a roller derby team.

Which is good because, while Cleveland is not the punchline it once was, it still comes in for a few lazy jabs. For example, Jimmy Fallon in February 2022 quipped, "I read that in the past few days, Elon Musk's net worth dropped below $200 billion. That's right, Elon Musk is no longer worth over $200 billion. Now when he flies to space, he has to connect in Cleveland. Sad."

Ba-dum-bump!

What Was League Park?

The first thing visitors to League Park notice is the right-field wall. It's ridiculously close to home plate, only 290 feet away. For comparison's sake, Progressive Field is 375 feet to right-center and 325 feet down the right-field line.

To compensate, League Park has a 40-foot-high wall in right field. Though it's now a see-through metal fence, back when major leaguers played here it was a wooden structure three feet higher than Fenway Park's famed Green Monster. Despite its height, the closeness of the wall made it an irresistible target for many batters, and right fielders had to learn to play caroms and ricochets off the wood.

League Park is a remnant of the early days of baseball before Major League Baseball enforced more uniformity on the game and the ballparks in which it's played. Located at East 66th Street and Lexington Avenue, it replaced two smaller parks on the East Side that both went by the name National League Park.

League Park was home to the Indians and their predecessors, the Spiders, as well as to the Buckeyes of the Negro American League and the NFL Cleveland Rams. It was home or visiting field to some of the greatest players in baseball history, including Babe Ruth, Bob Feller, Cy Young, Joe DiMaggio, and Ty Cobb.

League Park history

League Park was built as home field for the Cleveland Spiders, a National League baseball franchise. Opened in 1891, the wooden structure seated 9,000 with a single-deck grandstand behind home plate and a covered pavilion behind first base. The ballpark was rebuilt in concrete and steel for the 1910 season. A double-decker

League Park of yesteryear (left) blending into the park of today (right), at the corner of East 66th Street and Lexington Avenue. *Steve Kocevar*

grandstand and additional bleachers doubled the capacity to 18,000. At that time, the team was known as the Naps—in honor of player-manager Napoleon Lajoie. In 1915, the name changed again, this time to the Indians.

The field dimensions are so odd because League Park was built at a time when cities didn't bow to the wishes of stadium and team owners. If the builder wanted a new park, fine, but it had to fit the existing street grid. Right field had to be short because of Lexington Avenue, which carried streetcars that brought fans to the games.

In 1920, League Park was renamed Dunn Field in honor of team owner James Dunn, but it reverted to its original name in 1927.

By then, a new stadium was being built along the downtown lakefront. Cleveland Municipal Stadium, which opened in 1931, had the largest seating capacity of any outdoor arena in the world and was one of the first multipurpose stadiums.

The Indians played their first game there on July 31, 1932, and continued until the end of the 1933 season. Beginning in 1934, the team returned to League Park to play games on weekends and holidays until 1947. League Park's lack of lights was part of the reason the Indians moved for good.

Abandoned and rebuilt

Municipal Stadium, though it was home to the Indians for more than sixty years, was never really a baseball park. Cavernous and cold, subject to the winds off Lake Erie, it was always better suited for football. The Indians fled in 1994 for Jacobs Field (now Progressive Field), a smaller, brighter, and friendlier baseball-only park in the heart of the city. Municipal Stadium was torn down in 1997 to make way for a new football venue, Cleveland Browns Stadium.

League Park was mostly demolished in 1951 and the property turned into a playground. The only things that remained standing were the ticket house, built in 1909, and part of the grandstand wall along East 66th Street. Situated in the Hough neighborhood, the reduced state of the field was emblematic of the city's decline, particularly on the East Side.

In 1979, League Park was declared a Cleveland landmark and was placed on the National Register of Historic Places. But it wasn't until 2014 that the city restored the site, turning the ticket house into a home for the Baseball Heritage Museum and rebuilding the playing field with artificial turf for baseball games and recreation.

Great Moments in League Park History

Hall of Famer Cy Young pitched the first game on May 1, 1891.

Cleveland pitcher Addie Joss threw a perfect game on October 2, 1908, the fourth in Major League Baseball history.

The 1920 World Series, between the Indians and the Brooklyn Robins (Cleveland won the nine-game series).

Babe Ruth hit his 500th home run on August 11, 1929.

Joe DiMaggio gets a hit in his fifty-sixth consecutive game on July 16, 1941, setting a record that still stands. The streak would end the next day at Municipal Stadium.

Why Are There So Many Different Bridges Over the Cuyahoga?

Greater Clevelanders like to joke about sticking to their side of town and seldom visiting the other side, but if that were true, we wouldn't have so many bridges over the Cuyahoga River.

Stand almost anywhere downtown in sight of the river and you'll see bridges, lots of them, some just spanning the Cuyahoga River itself and others overarching the entire valley. Some move, some are fixed, and others were abandoned long ago.

To take a look at the subject of Cleveland bridges, let's start at ground level and work our way up.

Street-level bridges

The seven moveable bridges comprise one of the largest collection of such spans in the country, if not the world. Each of these bridges has an operator who sits in a control room, most of which are attached to the moving span, and monitors traffic and operates the structures. During the winter, when boat traffic is considerably less, one operator will manage multiple bridges, driving from one to the other to allow ships to pass.

Though they are an integral part of the city landscape, these bridges can be a problem. They are old and require frequent repairs, rebuilds, and even replacements that necessitate detours and hurt local businesses. Unexpected breakdowns can close a bridge for a day or even weeks while replacement parts are found or fashioned. Morning and evening commutes across the bridges are regularly interrupted by the *American Republic* or another freighter cautiously wending its way upstream or down.

From Lake Erie heading south, here are the movable bridges:

Norfolk Southern Railroad Bridge

Crossing the Cuyahoga near its mouth, this lift bridge is owned by the railroad and carries roughly one hundred trains a day. It is sometimes called the "Iron Curtain" because nothing of any size enters or exits the river until it is raised. It's the bane of summer boaters because when it's lowered, only kayakers and paddle-boarders can slip underneath. Rail traffic has priority, and that means everything from the *Goodtime III* to freighters must wait for the trains to pass and the bridge to lift out of the way. In response to criticism from boaters and businesses, the railroad in 2019 agreed to do a better job of keeping the bridge raised when there is no train coming.

Willow Avenue Lift Bridge

This bridge between the west bank of the Flats and Whiskey Island is the only one over the Old River Channel. It carries mostly truck traffic to and from businesses, including a crushed stone distributor and a salt mine beneath Lake Erie. However, a Metroparks pedestrian bridge that opened in 2021 over the Norfolk Southern tracks on Whiskey Island has increased the number of cyclists and walkers using the lift bridge. The city plans to replace the bridge with a higher, fixed span, which will mean one fewer movable bridge.

Center Street Bridge

This is the only bridge over the river that rotates horizontally rather than raises and lowers. It swings to the north to allow boat traffic to pass, then arcs back. Swing bridges used to be common on the river, but this one, built in 1901, is the only survivor. It was closed for an extensive rehabilitation that took all of 2022 and part of 2023.

Columbus Road Bridge

This is the location of the first permanent bridge over the

Cuyahoga. Originally covered (possibly the only covered bridge Cleveland ever had), it was the cause of the infamous Bridge War in 1836, which set residents of Cleveland and Ohio City (then a separate city) against each other in a fight over commercial traffic routes. The entire span was replaced in 2013. (The structure at that time dated to the 1940s.) The old span was lowered onto a barge and hauled away to be cut up for scrap.

Carter Road Bridge

Built in 1940, this bridge connects the northern tip of the Scranton Peninsula with the east bank of the Flats.

Nickle Plate Railroad Bridge

The original span, built in 1882, was the first high-level crossing of the river. It's the oldest operating rail line in the Cuyahoga Valley.

West 3rd Street Bridge

Built in 1940, it carries the trucks that service the terminals in the industrial heart of the valley.

High-level bridges

These bridges carry vehicular traffic into, out of, and through the city and are part of the principal commuter routes.

Main Avenue Bridge

Formally known as the Harold H. Burton Memorial Bridge, it joins the East Shoreway and West Shoreway on Ohio Route 2. At 8,000 feet in length, it is Ohio's longest elevated structure. Originally built in 1939, it underwent a major renovation in 1991.

Veterans Memorial Bridge

Opened in 1917 as the Detroit–Superior Bridge, it was the first high-level span for motor vehicles over the river. The lower deck once carried streetcars, which entered westbound at West 6th

A city of spans. *Shutterstock*

Street and Superior Avenue, and eastbound at West 25th Street and on Detroit Avenue. The streetcars stopped running in 1954. Since then, the lower deck has occasionally been opened for tours. It is considered by many to be the city's most attractive bridge.

Hope Memorial Bridge

Opened in 1932 as the Lorain–Carnegie Bridge and renamed in 1983 to honor comedian Bob Hope, this structure is best known for its four forty-two-foot art deco pylons, the Guardians of Traffic. These achieved greater prominence in 2021, when the Cleveland Indians baseball team, which plays in nearby Progressive Field, renamed itself the Guardians and appropriated the bridge's figures for its new logo.

Cuyahoga Viaduct

This structure carries the Greater Cleveland Regional Transit Authority's Red Line trains between Tower City and Cleveland Hopkins International Airport.

Inner Belt Bridge (George V. Voinovich Bridges)

Opened in 1959, these twin bridges are the main route into the city from the south and west, carrying I-90, I-71, and I-77 traffic. The aging structures were replaced with two new bridges in an enormous, traffic-snarling project from 2011 to 2016.

Farther to the south are the I-480 and Ohio Turnpike bridges over the river valley.

Abandoned Bridges

Although no longer used, these bridges remain part of the urban landscape. It's as if the city loves its bridges so much that it won't get rid of the ones it no longer needs. In some cases, only parts of the bridges remain as reminders of what once stood there.

Baltimore & Ohio Bascule Bridges

These two former railroad bascule bridges jut into the sky on the west bank of the Flats, the most prominent of Cleveland's abandoned bridges. Originally swing bridges like the Center Street span, they were built in the 1880s by the Valley Railway Co., crossing the Cuyahoga from Merwin Avenue to the west bank and then from the west bank over the Old River Channel to docks on Whiskey Island.

Because they required piers in the channel, these swing bridges narrowed the already tight river passage. The federal government ordered the Baltimore & Ohio to replace them with bascule bridges, which open and close like jackknives. The bascule bridges were then abandoned in 1984 when rail traffic declined. Bridge 464 is next to Shooter's on the Water. Bridge 463 looms over Jacobs Pavilion at Nautica, north of the Center Street Bridge. From the east bank you can still see where the bridge rested when it was in use.

Anyone who wants to see how a bascule bridge operates can find a working one crossing the Cuyahoga just north of the turning basin by the Cleveland-Cliffs steel mill south of I-490. Originally built in 1901, it's now owned by CSX.

Other Defunct Bridges

There are three abandoned lift bridges along the Cuyahoga's main channel:

1. Old River Road Bridge (between Columbus and Carter roads)
2. Old River Road Railroad Bridge (between Columbus and Carter roads)
3. Eagle Avenue Bridge (near the intersection of Carter and Scranton roads)

There are remnants on the west bank of two grand bridges long since demolished: the Central Viaduct and the Superior Viaduct.

Several stone pillars of the old Central Viaduct still stand on the west bank directly below the Innerbelt Bridge. The viaduct, which opened in 1888, was built with a swing span later replaced with an overhead truss in 1912. It was closed in 1941 and replaced by the Innerbelt Bridge.

The Superior Viaduct was the city's first great bridge. Opened in 1878, it lasted until 1920, when it was replaced by the Detroit-Superior Bridge. Its western approach still stands and is home to restaurants and apartments.

In the water, just upriver from the Hope Memorial Bridge, are two pylons from a former bridge made obsolete by the bigger span.

In total, the bridges—whether fixed or movable, high or low, in use or abandoned, carrying trains or vehicles—keep the city functioning while also rendering a unique cityscape.

Why Did the Browns
Move to Baltimore?

If Clevelanders were the forgiving sort, Art Modell would be a civic
hero.

Modell owned the Cleveland Browns for thirty-five years and
brought the city an NFL championship in 1964. He helped the NFL
become the entertainment behemoth it is today. He was a generous man and a supporter of the Cleveland Clinic and Hospice of
the Western Reserve, among other organizations.

But Modell is not revered in Cleveland. Far from it. The city
and team didn't hold a public memorial for him after he died. He
wasn't buried in Ohio. Even in death, Modell remains a pariah for
the unforgivable sin of moving the Browns to Baltimore in 1995.

Playing hardball

Why Modell turned his back on the city and moved the football team is a story of greed, politics, and political miscalculations.
While the late owner gets the primary blame, moving the team was
not as simple as Modell wanting more money and a new stadium.
And although the announcement stunned the city, the move was
years in the making.

Municipal Stadium was a hulking structure—the largest
outdoor arena in the world—when it opened in 1931 on reclaimed
land on the lakefront. Showing its age by the 1970s, it had fallen
well below the standards of other NFL stadiums. Cold and gray,
open to brutal winter winds off Lake Erie, it was a memorable, if
chilly, setting for football games, but a poor venue for Cleveland
Indians baseball.

In 1973, Modell signed a twenty-five-year lease with the city

Cleveland Municipal Stadium was vast and decrepit. Browns owner Art Modell wanted a new one. It didn't end well. This photo was taken during the stadium's final game on December 17, 1995. *Paul M. Walsh, via Wikimedia Commons / CC BY-SA 2.0*

to operate the stadium. In exchange for paying rent, his Stadium Corp. kept all revenues generated by the facility, including the sale of luxury suites that he added. He did not allow his tenant, the Indians, to share in that operating revenue, even though they generated some of it.

But Modell wanted more than a new lease; he really wanted a new stadium, one with loges and other amenities that would bring in additional revenue. He supported plans for a domed stadium, but voters rejected the proposal in 1984.

The Indians, tired of being Modell's tenants on a sublease, persuaded the county to put an issue on the ballot to build the Gateway complex, made up of a new ballpark for the Indians and an arena for the NBA Cavaliers, who would move downtown from Richfield Coliseum. Modell declined to participate in the project. He believed his financial position was secure where he was.

Betrayal

But after the Indians left for the new Jacobs Field in 1994, revenue at Municipal Stadium fell sharply. Modell, one of the least wealthy of NFL owners, convinced the county in 1995 to put a $175 million issue on the ballot to refurbish the aging stadium. He did not, however, wait for the outcome of the vote.

On November 6, 1995, at a press conference in Baltimore, Modell announced that he'd signed a deal to move the Browns. On the very next day, Cleveland voters approved the additional financing Modell said he needed to upgrade Municipal Stadium.

In addition to being financially pressed, Modell was worried about his legacy. He was getting older and wanted to hand down the team to his adopted son, David, rather than sell it. Unlike many NFL owners who made their fortunes elsewhere before buying teams, Modell became rich through ownership of the Browns. That also meant he didn't have a source of income apart from the team. The move to Baltimore meant additional revenue to keep the team and Modell's continued ownership viable.

For its part, Baltimore, which had had its heart ripped out when its beloved Colts were moved by their owner to Indianapolis in 1985, had no qualms about stabbing Cleveland in the back the same way it had been betrayed.

Fallout

The blowback to the proposed move was intense, even outside Cleveland. The Browns weren't the first NFL team to switch cities, but this jump felt particularly underhanded. On its cover, *Sports Illustrated* pictured a cartoon Modell sucker-punching a Browns fan. The City of Cleveland sued to block the move. Congress held hearings. Though a lot of people still felt sorry for Baltimore for losing the Colts, that city's willingness to steal a team from another city cost it any lingering sympathy.

Ultimately, the anti-move lawsuits were settled with an agreement that allowed Modell to move the team but forced him to surrender the name, team colors, and history. His Baltimore team would not be the Browns, but a new franchise (ultimately named the Ravens). After a three-year hiatus, Cleveland would get an expansion team—on the condition that it build a new stadium. The new team would assume the name, colors, and history of the Browns.

Though Modell was the villain in this drama, another man played a key behind-the-scenes role in moving the team. Al Lerner, the billionaire chairman of MBNA Corp., a large bank-holding company, was a minority owner of the Browns and advised Modell on the move, even acting as a go-between for the parties involved. The papers were signed on Lerner's private jet.

Then, Lerner quickly distanced himself from Modell, criticizing the move he'd helped negotiate.

In 1998, three years after the move was announced, Lerner (with Modell's support) was the successful bidder for the expansion team that would become the new Browns. He bid $530 million, at the time the highest price paid for a sports franchise. Lerner owned the team until his death in 2002 when it passed to his son, Randy. The younger Lerner, who seemed far more interested in his British soccer team, Aston Villa F.C., sold the Browns in 2012 to Jimmy and Dee Haslam for about $1 billion.

Legacy of the move

Was the move worth it for Modell?

He finally reached the Super Bowl in 2001 at age seventy-five when the Ravens beat the New York Giants. But despite the lucrative package he got for moving the team, Modell's financial problems did not go away. In 2000 the NFL pressured him into selling 49 percent of the team to businessman Steve Bisciotti, who purchased the remaining shares four years later.

David Modell was named president of the Ravens when they debuted in 1996 and stayed with the team through 2004. He died of lung cancer in 2017 at age fifty-five.

Art Modell's move triggered a spate of new stadium construction in the NFL as other owners used the threat of a move to extract funding from voters and local governments.

Despite his undeniable credentials and outstanding service to the league, Modell has not been selected to the NFL Hall of Fame and probably never will be, a snub that can be explained only by his decision to move the Browns.

The personal backlash against Modell was so severe that he

traveled with bodyguards and was never able to return to Cleveland. When he died in 2012 at age eighty-seven, he was buried in Maryland.

In a *cleveland.com* story after Modell's death, Kevin Byrne, who worked with him in Cleveland and Baltimore, said, "There was a lingering sadness, no doubt. I think he truly felt for the fans that he let them down because he couldn't make it work. He often second-guessed himself and said, 'Maybe I should've gone public with all the missed deadlines and broken promises.'"

As for Browns fans, as long as there are those who remember the move, Modell and the Ravens will be anathema.

"He died knowing the people of Cleveland despised him, and I can't imagine much worse than that," said Lee Weingart, a Cuyahoga County commissioner when the move happened.

What has made the hard feelings even worse for Clevelanders is the success of the Ravens compared to the Browns. After relocating, the Ravens became regular playoff contenders and won two Super Bowls. By contrast, the expansion Browns became one of the most hapless teams in the NFL and made the playoffs only twice in twenty-four years. The fact that both teams play in the AFC North means Cleveland is reminded twice a season of the Ravens' superiority and Modell's treachery.

Why Does Cleveland Party So Hard On St. Patrick's Day?

Every March 17th, Cleveland throws itself an epic party centered around the St. Patrick's Day parade downtown.

Superior Avenue from East 21st Street to Public Square is lined three-deep with spectators for the parade. Those unfortunate enough to have to work that day share sidewalks with revelers sporting green hair and an endless variety of T-shirts proclaiming their affinity for Ireland, the Irish, green beer, and corned beef. (Slyman's Restaurant and Deli on St. Clair Avenue alone sells 2,000 to 3,000 corned beef sandwiches that day.)

The celebration is not confined to downtown. Bars throughout Northeast Ohio open early on St. Patrick's Day.

"In the eyes of a lot of people, it's a holiday. They don't go to work, that's for sure," said John O'Brien, president of the West Side Irish American Club.

According to one travel site, Cleveland's is the ninth-largest parade and party in the country. Other cities that do it up in a big way: New York, Boston, Chicago, and Savannah, Georgia.

Why is it such a party here?

It can't be attributed entirely to the Irish Americans. While they're one of the largest ethnic groups in Northeast Ohio, they're not the biggest. (That title is saved for the Germans). And a casual scan of the crowds along the parade route and in bars makes it clear that the celebration is not limited to those of Irish descent.

St. Patrick's Day might be a big deal because it also serves as an end-of-winter rite, a way to celebrate surviving another Northeast Ohio deep freeze and to welcome spring—even though warm weather and daffodils might be weeks away.

Looks like fun, but don't count on being comfortable in just shirtsleeves in Cleveland in March. *Erik Drost, via Flickr / CC BY 2.0*

And, like Cinco de Mayo, the day has been appropriated by the general public as an excuse for a party. After the big year-end holidays, winter is largely free of celebrations that lend themselves to parties, so St. Patrick's Day is the first chance since New Year's Eve to let loose.

"A lot of people think St. Patrick's Day means winter is over and spring is here," O'Brien said. "It really isn't true, but there's no harm in thinking that way."

Whatever Happened to Michigan Avenue?

There's Ontario Street, Huron Road, Erie Court, and Superior Avenue—that's four out of the five Great Lakes represented in the downtown street grid. So where's the road named for Michigan?

Did the early settlers somehow have a premonition of the football rivalry that would develop between Ohio and Michigan and decide to preemptively snub the State Up North? That would have been the better story, but, sadly, the answer is no.

Cleveland did once have a Michigan Avenue, but it was obliterated to make way for construction of the Terminal Tower complex from 1927 to 1930. I guess if a street had to go, that was the one.

Why Does Cleveland Keep Losing Population?

In 1930, Cleveland was the sixth-largest city in the country. Its population of 900,429 put it behind New York, Chicago, Philadelphia, Detroit, and Los Angeles. And the city wasn't finished growing; its population peaked in 1950 at 914,808. Since then, though, Cleveland's population has declined steeply, falling to 372,624 in 2020—a level it last saw in the early 1900s.

Cleveland is now the fifty-fourth largest city in the U.S., behind such relatively anonymous towns as Aurora, Colorado, and Mesa, Arizona. It's no longer even the biggest city in Ohio; Columbus is more than twice as populous at 905,748.

Of course, the city of Cleveland's population is only part of the region's demographic whole. Cleveland and Cuyahoga County are part of the Cleveland–Elyria Metropolitan Statistical Area (MSA), which also includes the counties of Geauga, Lake, Lorain, and Medina. Its 2020 population of 2,043,807 made it the thirty-fourth most populous MSA in the country. While the MSA population loss has not been as steep as that of the city, it's also been on the downturn. The Cleveland MSA now trails those of Columbus (32nd) and Cincinnati (30th).

Cleveland is not alone in this decline. Most Rust Belt cities have lost residents since factories closed, industries fled, and workers followed jobs to the Sunbelt. Pittsburgh, Buffalo, Detroit, Youngstown, and other cities also shrunk.

The decline in population has been devastating to Cleveland. A smaller population means fewer resources, less revenue, a greater burden on the remaining residents, and declining influence at the state and federal levels. There's also the loss of prestige. Having fallen from the sixth-largest city in the country to the second-largest in Ohio, Cleveland is not what it once was.

Remnants of Cleveland's more populous past are everywhere: in the wide traffic arteries, like Superior Avenue; in the three major league sports teams (the smallest city to have MLB, NFL, and NBA franchises); and in cultural and arts institutions, like the Cleveland Orchestra and the Cleveland Museum of Art, both of which were founded when the city was bigger and more prosperous.

As the city shrinks, it's fair to wonder if it can continue to support these cultural legacies. Financial difficulties forced the Cleveland Ballet to move to San Jose, California, in 2004 (though another company has since taken its place), and the Cleveland Orchestra in 2007 began an annual winter residency in Miami.

An exodus to the suburbs

Though people tend to think of Cleveland's population decline as a relatively recent trend, it actually began in 1940. It accelerated in the 1950s as thousands of homes were built in Euclid, Parma, South Euclid, and other inner-ring suburbs to accommodate World War II veterans and the families they started. The makeup of the city was changing as well. Native and foreign-born White residents were moving out; Black people and southern Whites were moving in.

The loss of city residents to the suburbs is reflected in the percentage of county population that lives in Cleveland: In 1950, Cleveland represented 66 percent of Cuyahoga County's population; by 2020 it had declined to 29 percent.

Population patterns in Cleveland and other cities that have lost residents follow a wave of people looking for a better place to live, leaving behind neighborhoods in which they no longer wanted to stay. As various ethnic groups became wealthier and more assimilated, they moved out for better living conditions.

The region's Jewish population is an example. Originally based in the Central Market area just southeast of Public Square, the center of Cleveland's Jewish community then moved to the Glenville, Kinsman, and Hough neighborhoods. During the 1940s through the 1960s, much of the Jewish population shifted east to Shaker Heights, Cleveland Heights, and University Heights. The eastward move continued into Solon, Orange, Pepper Pike, and Beachwood, the latter of which now has one of the highest per capita concentrations of Jews outside of Israel, according to the *Cleveland Jewish News.*

The Laws of Housing Dynamics

No one has spent more time studying housing and population trends in Northeast Ohio than Thomas Bier, Ph.D., a senior fellow at Cleveland State University's Maxine Goodman Levin College of Urban Affairs and former director of the Center for Housing Research and Policy.

In his 2017 book, *Housing Dynamics in Northeast Ohio: Setting the Stage for Resurgence,* Bier attributes the city's population loss and subsequent decline to four Laws of Housing Dynamics, summarized below:

First Law of Housing Dynamics: People move, and when they do, most move "up" to a property that is newer and higher priced—which means the mainstream of movement across all communities is toward newer places and away from older ones.

Second Law of Housing Dynamics: Most buildings have a lifespan. They age, become obsolete, and are demolished. Properties in lowest demand in the market place are the ones closest to the end of their lifespan. However, properties that receive high-quality maintenance can have their life extended indefinitely.

Third Law of Housing Dynamics: The market-driven construction of housing can result in an oversupply for the region—that is, more houses and apartments exist than households to occupy all of them. Oversupply forces vacancy and abandonment among the least desirable properties in the region. Another aspect of market-driven construction is "urban sprawl."

Fourth Law of Housing Dynamics: Government, particularly the state, strongly influences the functioning of the first three laws by favoring some communities over others, giving them a competitive advantage. It is in the interest of the disfavored communities to perceive and overcome this disadvantage.

A struggling school system, crime, and a decline in public services also contribute to the exodus of residents. However, for Bier, it's the economy. Cleveland and the region simply haven't been able to modernize and diversify thoroughly and quickly enough to keep up with the digital economy. As a result, it has suffered accordingly.

Can population loss be stopped?

How to slow, stop, and ultimately reverse population loss has been the subject of a great deal of study and civic teeth-gnashing. Organizations like Destination Cleveland, Engage! Cleveland and Greater Cleveland Partnership have made it a priority, but while population loss has slowed, it hasn't been stopped, let alone reversed.

Some say Cleveland should annex some suburbs, like East Cleveland, for the population boost, or that the city and county should merge to form a new metropolis that would be the tenth largest in the country. Either option would require voter approval, and that seems unlikely.

Much of the planning around stopping population loss has centered on bringing an end to the so-called "brain drain," the loss of Greater Cleveland's educated young people to other regions. But that requires creating enough attractive, high-paying, professional jobs in the area to keep them—something the city has struggled to do.

There also have been efforts to attract transplants from other parts of the country, whether they're homesick former Clevelanders wanting to start families in familiar surroundings or people fleeing high rents and home prices in Brooklyn or San Diego.

The rise of remote work means digital employees can live almost anywhere. Leaders hope people will choose to locate in less expensive and more "livable" cities like Cleveland even if they're working for firms in Chicago or New York.

Some people think the region's access to fresh water in Lake Erie ultimately will reverse the exodus and bring drought-stricken Arizonans and Nevadans to our shores.

Others are convinced that the answer lies in attracting international immigrants and refugees, noting the region's strong ethnic enclaves, rich history of immigration, and the economic boost that immigrants can bring.

Cleveland was once a primary destination for immigrants. Coming in waves, first from Germany and Ireland, then from southern and Eastern Europe, they built the city, manned its factories, and started businesses. In 1900, roughly 30 percent of the city's population was foreign-born; 120 years later, that number was about 4 percent.

What does the future hold?

Bier is pessimistic about Cleveland's chances of regaining population. In fact, population loss has spread to the inner-ring suburbs. East Cleveland is the most extreme example, but Euclid, South Euclid, Brook Park, Warrensville Heights, and other communities are losing population. and their housing stock is declining.

"Economic strength shifts toward the new," Bier said in an interview. "The momentum is always toward the new and renewed property. To change that requires very powerful forces that communities on their own are unable to produce."

The revitalization of city neighborhoods such as Tremont, Ohio City, North Collinwood, and Detroit-Shoreway is encouraging but unlikely to compensate for population loss, he said.

If there is a bright spot in all the population reports, it's that Cleveland has steadily grown its downtown population to an estimated fifteen thousand in 2020. That growth has helped revitalize downtown as a residential area, though it has not been enough to offset the population loss elsewhere.

The region's best hope is to adopt a tax-sharing plan similar to the one in the Minneapolis–St. Paul region, Bier said. In that system, communities experiencing business growth share a portion of their property tax base with cities that are not as prosperous.

"That's the answer." Bier said. "Is that likely (here)? No."

Cleveland Population

1900—381,768	1980—573,822
1920—796,841	2000—477,472
1940—878,336	2020—372,624
1960—876,050	

Cuyahoga County Population

1900—439,120	1980—1,498,400
1920—943,495	2000—1,393,978
1940—1,217,250	2020—1,264,817
1960—1,647,895	

Why Is A Christmas Story Such a Big Deal in Cleveland?

Ask Greater Clevelanders to name their favorite Christmas movie, and some will say *Elf* or *It's A Wonderful Life*. But most are likely to answer with *A Christmas Story*, a 1983 film that has cemented its place in the hearts of Cleveland residents.

Walk down any Greater Cleveland street in December and you'll see a leg lamp in at least one front window. Drop "It's a major award!", "Bumpuses!", "Fra*jee*lay," or "Fuuudge!" into a conversation and you'll be rewarded with knowing laughs. For fans, the annual TV movie marathon beginning on Christmas Eve is as much a part of the holiday as opening presents and decorating trees.

But why?

The movie isn't set in Cleveland. It takes place in fictional 1940s Hohman, Indiana, itself a stand-in for Hammond, Indiana, the hometown of author Jean Shepherd, whose short stories inspired the film.

And it wasn't entirely filmed here, either. Much of the film was shot in Ontario, Canada, including the school and tree-shopping scenes, though Cleveland's Public Square and Higbee's department store are featured prominently.

Clevelanders' affection for *A Christmas Story* is centered on a house on West 11th Street in Tremont. The modest structure was used primarily for its exterior as home to the movie's Parker family. (Interior scenes were shot in Canada.)

The building is now The Christmas Story House and Museum, a faithful rendering of the house—down to the yellow siding, green trim, and leg lamp in the front window. The interior was exten-

"Bumpuses!" Fans of *A Christmas Story* line up in Tremont.
Tim Evanson, via Flickr / CC BY-SA 2.0

sively remodeled to replicate the movie set. It's open year-round and can even be reserved for overnight stays.

Brian Jones, whose lifelong obsession with the movie led him to buy the house and remodel the interior in 2006 to match the movie set, attributes the popularity of the film among locals to its ties to the city, even though Cleveland isn't mentioned once in the film (except for the incidental detail that the family lives on Cleveland Street).

Hundreds of Higbee's department store employees participated in the movie's epic parade and visit with Santa scenes. Shots of the store's windows along Public Square are nostalgia to those old enough to remember Higbee's and nearby Halle's annual holiday displays.

"People still come up to me and tell me they were an extra in the movie," Jones said.

The movie's shots in Tremont capture a Cleveland that is both vanished, yet somehow still very much alive.

"Clevelanders just identify with the movie," Jones said. "I don't think I could have pulled this off in any other city."

What many forget are the three sequels to *A Christmas Story*. The first, *My Summer Story,* premiered in 1994. Like the original, it is narrated by Jean Shepherd, but the parts were all recast: Charles Grodin as The Old Man, Mary Steenburgen as Mrs. Parker, and Kieran Culkin as Ralphie. Even though most of that movie was shot in Cleveland in the summer of 1993, it never achieved the status of the original.

A Christmas Story 2, released in 2012, went straight to DVD. It starred Daniel Stern as The Old Man and Braeden Lemasters as Ralphie. Filmed in British Columbia, it got mostly negative reviews.

In late 2022, *A Christmas Story Christmas* was released starring Peter Billingsley, who played Ralphie Parker in the original. It features an adult Ralphie in the 1970s. The movie was shot in Hungary.

Notable Movies Filmed in Northeast Ohio

Air Force One (1997)	*The Fate of the Furious* (2017)
Alex Cross (2012)	*The Fortune Cookie* (1966)
American Splendor (2003)	*The Kid from Cleveland* (1949)
Antwone Fisher (2002)	*The Land* (2016)
The Avengers (2012)	*Light of Day* (1987)
Captain America: The Winter Soldier (2014)	*My Friend Dahmer* (2017)
	Spider Man 3 (2007)
A Christmas Story (1983)	*Stranger Than Paradise* (1984)
The Deer Hunter (1978)	*Welcome to Collinwood* (2002)
Draft Day (2014)	*White Noise* (2022)

Why Is Burke Lakefront Airport Still There, Taking Up All that Prime Lakefront Property?

Burke Lakefront Airport occupies 450 acres of some of the most desirable real estate in the Midwest. The notion that the land could serve a better purpose than as a lightly used airport has been around for decades, but until recently, no serious steps have been taken to close Burke.

The future of the airport and the land remains one of the most hotly debated questions in the city. To understand why Burke has become such a hotpoint, it's necessary to know why the airport came to be built and how it's used now.

Designated reliever

When Cleveland Hopkins International Airport opened in 1925, already there was discussion of the need for a second airport on the downtown lakefront. However, operations didn't begin on the first lakefront runway—made of dirt—until 1947. Subsequent city administrations added landfill to make room for two hard surface runways, a control tower, a passenger terminal, hangars, and more. Originally named Municipal Airport, in 1960 it was renamed in honor of former mayor and U.S. senator Thomas Burke.

Various small commercial airlines flew out of Burke, serving midwestern cities from the 1950s until the 1980s, when commercial air service from the smaller airport became less profitable and was largely discontinued. Since then, most air traffic at Burke has been general aviation, mostly private pilots and corporate jets. The airport is also home to several flight schools and the International Women's Air & Space Museum.

In the past few decades, more people have been to Burke as spectators than as passengers.

Since 1964, Burke has hosted the Cleveland National Air Show, a Labor Day tradition highlighted by appearances from the U.S. Navy's Blue Angels or U.S. Air Force's Thunderbirds aerobatic teams. The fact that Burke can be shut down to host the air show weakens the argument that it is needed relief for Hopkins.

In the same vein, every summer from 1982 to 2007, Burke hosted an open-wheel auto race, known originally as the Cleveland Budweiser 500, then the Cleveland Grand Prix, and, finally, the Grand Prix of Cleveland.

Though the Federal Aviation Administration (FAA) still designates Burke as a reliever airport for Hopkins, the need for that backup has lessened, if not completely disappeared. Air traffic at Hopkins has declined, particularly since the merger of Continental and United Airlines led to the elimination of the combined company's Cleveland hub in 2014.

Flight operations at Burke have been in a tailspin for decades. The total number of operations in 2020 was 30,794, down 42 percent since 2010. And those operations numbers were artificially inflated with the flight schools' practice takeoffs and landings included in the count.

Lakefront development

Some civic leaders and organizations in recent years have tried to undo disastrous earlier decisions regarding lakefront access, working to reopen for public-use land that has for decades been closed off by highways, railroads, and private ownership. Progress, although substantial, has been slow and piecemeal.

For proponents of lakefront development, Burke is prize property. Converting the airport to some mix of public and private use could link Edgewater on the west to East 55th Street on the east (with some notable gaps).

Those who would close Burke argue that its benefits for Cleveland are minimal and declining, and the city would fare better putting that lakefront property to another use.

None of the arguments for keeping the airport make sense

It might be landfill, but that's still a lot of valuable lakefront. Many people consider Burke Lakefront Airport to be lost opportunity. *Tim Evanson, via Flickr / CC BY-SA 2.0*

logistically or economically, said Robert Simons, a professor at the Maxine Goodman Levin College of Urban Affairs at Cleveland State University.

Closing Burke and either selling or developing the site could earn the city much-needed revenue instead of being a drain on the budget, said Simons, who specializes in urban development and even taught a course on redevelopment of Burke.

"It loses money, and it has a huge (lost) opportunity cost," he said.

The FAA's role

Decommissioning Burke isn't entirely up to the City of Cleveland; the FAA has the final say—and the agency doesn't like to close airports. But that doesn't mean it can't happen.

The Santa Monica Airport in Southern California, which is much busier than Burke, is scheduled to close at the end of 2028 to make way for a park. Blue Ash Airport near Cincinnati closed in 2012 and is now an industrial park.

The city of Chicago infamously did not wait for FAA permission to close its lakefront airport.

Meigs Field was a single-runway airport on the shores of Lake

Michigan. Like Burke, it served primarily the downtown business district. By 1955, it was the busiest single-runway airport in the country.

But in 1994, the city and the Chicago Park District, which owned the land, tried to replace it with a park. It was temporarily closed in the winter of 1996–97, but the Illinois Legislature forced the city to reopen it. In 2001, the city, state, and other parties agreed to keep Meigs open for another twenty-five years, but then promised federal funding fell through.

Finally, Mayor Richard Daley had had enough. On the night of March 30, 2003, he ordered city bulldozers to gouge Xs into the runway, making it unusable and thus effectively closing the airport in violation of the agreement and FAA rules.

Despite efforts to force its reopening, Meigs remained closed. Chicago paid a fine and repaid some FAA grants but won in the end. Northerly Island, where Meigs once operated, is now a 119-acre park.

Without such drastic action, closing Burke would be a long, arduous process that would take over a decade, but it will not begin without a request from the city. During his four terms in office, Mayor Frank Jackson never pursued closing Burke and the possibilities for redevelopment of the site. However, Mayor Justin Bibb, after taking office in 2022, hired a consultant to study decommissioning the airport.

Local hospital systems have opposed the move, saying a downtown airport is crucial to arriving organ donations.

Making the case

Even if the city requests the closure of Burke, the FAA places conditions on closure. Cleveland would have to prove to the agency's satisfaction that Burke is no longer needed as a reliever for Hopkins. A big part of that argument would be that the role could be filled by Cuyahoga County Regional Airport in Richmond Heights, which largely caters to corporate air travel.

The City of Cleveland would claim that the airport is too expensive to maintain and that the land could be put to better use. The local congressional delegation and Ohio senators would be asked to pressure the FAA. Lastly, the city would have to reimburse the agency a portion of the millions of dollars in grants made to Burke over the decades.

The airport sits within the ward of Councilman Kerry McCormack. One of the loudest voices for closing Burke, McCormack welcomed the new administration's willingness to explore another use for the property.

"Burke Lakefront Airport is a complete leech on our airport system. There is a mountain of evidence for closing it," he said, noting that the cost of supporting Burke requires higher landing fees at Hopkins, which means more expensive flights.

The city should keep ownership of the property and ensure that whatever development takes place includes public access to the lakefront, McCormack said.

He is not deterred by how long it might take to close Burke. "Hard things are hard and they take time," he said. "The only thing this is going to take is the political will to do it."

Why Is Cleveland Among the Nation's Poorest Cities?

For suburbanites whose trips to Cleveland are limited to downtown or a handful of entertainment districts, the city's extreme poverty is, to a degree, invisible. Cleveland's poorest neighborhoods don't draw a lot of visitors.

To the casual eye, the city can look prosperous—the result of recent construction projects downtown and aging office buildings turned into high-priced apartments. But the poverty is there, just a few blocks away.

The U.S. Census Bureau in 2022 declared Cleveland the second-poorest big city in the nation, next to Detroit. Its poverty rate of 29.2 percent meant about 114,000 residents were living in poverty, including 37,000 children.

Why is Cleveland so poor?

Many causes, few solutions

The answers are myriad. Cleveland, like much of the Rust Belt, suffered serious economic hardship in the 1970s and 1980s as jobs fled to the Sun Belt and overseas. Fortune 500 companies merged with others or moved their headquarters elsewhere. The North American Free Trade Agreement (NAFTA), which took effect in 1994, compounded job loss.

Northeast Ohio was particularly susceptible to disruption because its economy was built on the hard-hit industries of automotive, steel, and machine parts manufacturing, said Claudia Coulton, director of the Center for Urban Poverty and Community Development at Case Western Reserve University.

The region was slow to invest in the new tech economy, instead focusing on mostly futile efforts to land one more auto plant or manufacturer, clinging to the past rather than focusing on the future, said John Corlett, president and executive director of The Center for Community Solutions.

Though the regional economy has diversified somewhat, with healthcare gaining new prominence, the manufacturing base has never recovered. Other cities, including rival Pittsburgh, have proven more nimble in adapting to the demands of the high-tech economy.

Unlike the old blue-collar union jobs, which offered workers a comfortable living with a high school degree, the new jobs being created are more likely to require a college degree.

And therein lies another problem. Ohio trails the national average in percentage of adults with four-year degrees, and Cleveland lags behind the rest of Ohio. A 2021 study from WalletHub ranked Ohio as twenty-ninth of fifty states in educational attainment, and Greater Cleveland as eighty-sixth among U.S. metros. That lack of education creates a mismatch between the available work and the available labor pool, Coulton said.

In addition, the decline of unions has resulted in lower wages, fewer benefits, and the elimination of pensions, all of which have hurt incomes.

Racism at the root

Coulton and Corlett also blame racism and segregation for much of the region's economic woes.

"You look at the history of the city and see how much of it is guided by racism," Corlett said. "Segregation is one of those things that drive poverty in a community."

In the 1960s and 1970s, integration and forced busing caused working- and middle-class Whites to move out of the city, leaving behind Black residents, who tended to be poorer. Discriminatory lending practices by banks made it difficult for Black people to buy homes and begin to accumulate generational wealth.

The one-two punch of the housing crisis and the Great Recession of 2007–10 staggered the local economy further. "We haven't been able to reverse the process," Coulton said.

Will Cleveland ever stop vying with Detroit for the title of poorest big city? It's hard to say. Growth in the downtown population helps, but it is not enough to reverse the city's fortunes.

Coulton and Corlett say real help must come at the federal level: in the form of trade policies that are more favorable to manufacturing; from expansion of the federal Child Tax Credit; and from innovative antipoverty programs such as Universal Basic Income.

"We can't put it on the cities to have those policies. That has to be nationwide," Coulton said.

Cleveland's Poorest Neighborhoods by Median Household Income

1. Central ($10,441)
2. University ($17,195)
3. Kinsman ($18,046)
4. Buckeye-Woodhill ($18,186)
5. Hough ($19,003)
6. Fairfax ($20,332)
7. St. Clair–Superior ($22,962)
8. Cuyahoga Valley ($23,061)
9. Goodrich–Kirtland Park ($24,964)
10. Euclid-Green ($25,956)

Source: Center for Community Solutions, compiled from results of the U.S. Census Bureau's 2019 American Community Survey, via Cleveland.com

Why Does the East Side Get More Snow?

How tough a winter you endure in Cleveland depends to a large degree on where you live.

Every Greater Clevelander knows that the East Side gets more snow than the West and that a swath of the East Side known as the Snow Belt gets the most of all.

But how much more snow does the East Side get? Official National Weather Service snow totals for Cleveland are measured at Cleveland Hopkins International Airport, which is often misleading. The airport is on the West Side and miles from Lake Erie, which means it regularly gets less snow than other areas, particularly the East Side.

While there are no official figures comparing the two sides of town, it's not uncommon for Lakewood to receive two inches of snow, while on the East Side, the Heights and Chardon shovel out from six inches or more. Cleveland gets an average of 60-65 inches a year while Chardon has to deal with 107 inches.

Why the difference? It's geography.

The Lake Effect

Prevailing winds in Cleveland generally blow out of the west or northwest as they cross Lake Erie. When the lake is not fully frozen, the wind picks up moisture that it then drops in the form of snow.

And because the coastline east of the Cuyahoga River juts northeast, the East Side is squarely in the path of those moisture-laden clouds. That's why the counties of Lake, Ashtabula, and Geauga routinely lead the entire state in snow accumulation.

Elevation also contributes. The clouds drop snow as the winds are forced upward, and the East Side is generally higher than the West Side and the lakeshore. Of course, in Ohio, "high ground" is relative. Most of the city of Cleveland sets at 653 feet above sea level while Chardon is at a lofty 1,299 feet.

While the term "snow belt" is frequently used, there is no agreement on its exact boundaries. The most generous description is the eastern half of Cuyahoga County and all of Geauga, Lake, and Ashtabula counties, as well as the northwestern corner of Pennsylvania—and, of course, Buffalo.

It's cold comfort to Northeast Ohioans on a February morning while shoveling out of the driveway to know that "lake effect" snowbelts are rare. Yet it's true. Only two such regions exist in the entire United States: ours (south of Lake Erie and east of Cleveland) and another one (south of Lake Ontario stretching from Rochester to Watertown, New York).

The frequency and amount of lake-effect snow depends to a degree on the amount of ice on Lake Erie. The more surface covered by ice, the less moisture the winds can pick up, so an iced-over lake shuts off the lake-effect snow machine.

The worst blizzards

Not every snowfall in Northeast Ohio includes lake-effect snow, and not every lake-effect snowfall is heavy. But sometimes the results can be staggering. Everyone who has lived in Greater Cleveland for any length of time has their own experience with a memorable storm (or entire winter).

Among the worst was the Thanksgiving Blizzard of 1950, which lasted five days and dropped 22 inches of snow on Cleveland, accompanied by single-digit temperatures and 60 mph winds. The Ohio National Guard used tanks and bulldozers to battle 20-foot-high drifts and rescue stranded motorists. Schools remained closed for the week. In the end, twenty-three lives were lost.

The worst blizzard in Cleveland history hit on January 26, 1978. Two low-pressure fronts combined to form a winter cyclone that lowered the barometer to a record 28.26 inches. The temperature dropped by 39 degrees in six hours. Winds blew 53 mph with 82 mph gusts as the wind chill exceeded -100 F, and eight inches of snow fell.

Hopkins Airport closed because of zero visibility. The entire Ohio Turnpike was shut down for the first time ever, and 110,000 Greater Cleveland homes lost power. The blizzard, the third major storm of the winter of 1977–78, paralyzed much of the eastern U.S. and was the lowlight of Cleveland's second-snowiest winter.

While there is no avoiding winter in Northeast Ohio, living on the West Side can make it more bearable.

How Did the Cleveland Orchestra Get to Be World Famous?

Even in Cleveland's darkest days, when the Cuyahoga River burned and Johnny Carson made the city a nightly punchline, locals could point to one thing with pride: the Cleveland Orchestra.

Along with the orchestras in Boston, Philadelphia, Chicago, and New York, it's one of the "Big Five" of American symphonic music. In October 2020, an article in the *New York Times* claimed, "The Cleveland Orchestra is America's finest, still." The Cleveland Orchestra regularly tours to rapturous reviews in European music capitals and is routinely ranked among the greatest in the world.

Even those who slammed Cleveland in the 1970s acknowledged its orchestra's greatness in one of the common putdowns of the city:

Q: What's the difference between Cleveland and the Titanic?
A: Cleveland's got a better orchestra.

How did the orchestra become so good and, more confounding, remain so good even as the city declined around it?

Humble beginnings

If the orchestra now seems too grand, too accomplished, for a second-tier city like Cleveland, it's important to remember that it got its start at a time when Cleveland was growing rapidly and had viable aspirations of taking its place among the major cities of the country.

The Cleveland Orchestra defends its spot in the "Big Five" at Severance Hall.
Roger Mastroianni, courtesy of Cleveland Orchestra

The orchestra was founded by impresario Adella Prentiss Hughes, a classically trained pianist who managed a series of concerts that brought some of the nation's best orchestral music to Cleveland. In 1915, she helped found the Musical Arts Association, which presented concerts and opera, including a performance of Wagner's *Siegfried,* at League Park, home of the Cleveland Indians.

Hughes was instrumental in assembling an orchestra for a 1918 concert at Grays Armory to benefit St. Ann Catholic Church in Cleveland Heights. The young orchestra was ambitious from the start, traveling to New York City in 1922 to play at Carnegie Hall. Two years later, it issued its first recording, a shortened version of Tchaikovsky's *1812 Overture.*

"Second to none"

While the orchestra had built a solid reputation, it did not begin its ascent to the top ranks until George Szell became music director. The Hungarian-born Szell is generally regarded as one of the finest conductors of the twentieth century. His perfectionism was legendary. During his first season with the orchestra in 1946, he dismissed twelve of the ninety-four musicians. An unrelenting taskmaster, he took the orchestra to unprecedented musical heights and built its prestige by extending the season, improving Severance Hall acoustics, increasing musician pay, and taking it on European tours.

In 1967, it became the first American orchestra to be invited to the premiere festivals in Salzburg, Lucerne, and Edinburgh in the same summer. Szell also supervised the opening of the orchestra's summer home, Blossom Music Center, in 1968. That created full-time employment for musicians, which made it easier for the orchestra to hire the best.

Even as Cleveland slumped in the 1960s and 1970s, the orchestra remained excellent, an oasis in a bleak urban landscape.

After Szell's death in 1970, he was succeeded by the brilliant Lorin Maazel, who led the orchestra for ten years. The two subsequent music directors, Christoph von Dohnanyi and Franz Welser-Most, each put their own stamp on the orchestra without diminishing its greatness.

A hall like no other

The orchestra's history cannot be separated from that of its home for nearly one hundred years: Severance Hall.

From its founding in 1918, the Cleveland Orchestra played primarily at Masonic Auditorium (on Euclid Avenue at East 36th Street), which was not designed for symphonic music. By the end of the 1920s, the Musical Arts Association began fundraising for a permanent home. Board President John Severance and his wife, Elisabeth, pledged $1 million. The Western Reserve Society donated the land, and other civic heavyweights, including John D. Rockefeller, Dudley Blossom, and William Bingham, contributed as well.

The $7 million raised paid for the building and an endowment. When it opened in 1931, the building included an 1,800-seat concert hall, a 400-seat chamber music hall, a 6,000-pipe organ, and a recording studio. The stage was rebuilt in 1958 to improve acoustics.

Though regarded as one of the most beautiful concert halls in the country, it deteriorated somewhat over the years and lost some of its elegance until, in 1998, it underwent a two-year, $36 million renovation that enhanced the acoustics and restored the original detailing.

Since being restored, Severance Hall has regained its stature as one of the country's finest classical music venues.

In 2021, the orchestra changed the name of its home to Severance Music Center in response to a $50 million grant from the Jack, Joseph and Morton Mandel Foundation, the largest gift in orchestra history and one of the largest an orchestra has ever received. The hall in which the orchestra plays was named the Mandel Concert Hall.

Deserving of each other

Great orchestras are both self-perpetuating and in need of constant maintenance and reinforcement. That's not as contradictory as it seems. They're self-perpetuating because they're able to attract the best musicians, get invited to tour, perform at prestigious music festivals around the world, and record. Being a member of the Cleveland Orchestra would be the pinnacle of almost any musician's career.

And they're also in need of constant attention because anything excellent can deteriorate, for both artistic and financial reasons. The fact that the Cleveland Orchestra has not lost its luster is a tribute to both itself and the city that it calls home.

In his definitive history of the symphony, *The Cleveland Orchestra Story,* classical music critic Donald Rosenberg put it this way:

That Cleveland has deserved, and continues to deserve, its world-class orchestra cannot be questioned. The confluence of an industrial city, bold artistic and business leaders, superior musicians, and devoted audiences has brought about a remark-able music phenomenon. Throughout its history, the Cleveland Orchestra has reflected a community's ability to sustain . . . something fine and beautiful.

Cleveland Orchestra Timeline

1918—First performance
1922—First radio broadcast
1924—First recording (Tchaikovsky's *1812 Overture*)
1931—Severance Hall opens
1946—George Szell becomes conductor
1964—Blossom Music Center opens
1972—Lorin Maazel becomes conductor
1984—Christoph von Dohnanyi becomes conductor
1992—First American orchestra to establish residency at Salzburg Festival
2000—Residency in Miami begins; Severance Hall renovated
2002—Franz Welser-Most becomes conductor

Where's Our Domed Stadium?

Winter weather on Cleveland's lakefront can be awful. Any fan who's suffered through below-zero windchills and 30 mph gusts off Lake Erie has wondered why he or she couldn't be watching the Browns play indoors.

The Weather Channel has ranked Cleveland as the third-worst weather city in the NFL, behind only Green Bay and Buffalo, citing snow, wind, and temperatures as contributing factors. Perhaps no game epitomized the worst of Browns weather better than the 1981 AFC Divisional Playoff with the Oakland Raiders. The temperature was -5 degrees with windchills into the -20s. The awful weather was one of the reasons the Browns attempted a pass rather than a field goal on the last drive of the game. The resulting interception and loss lives on in the memories of Browns fans as the "Red Right 88" game.

Plenty of plans, but little action

It's not like the city hasn't tried to move the game indoors. Civic leaders started talking about a domed stadium in the 1960s, but the idea didn't garner serious attention until the early 1980s, a perilous time for Cleveland sports.

The Browns and Indians were playing in Municipal Stadium, an aging facility that fell well short of the requirements for modern sports franchises. The Cavs' home was Richfield Coliseum, on a piece of prairie halfway between Cleveland and Akron. A group of public officials led by County Commissioner Vincent Campanella imagined bringing all three teams together at a single location downtown. Browns owner Art Modell liked the idea, and a property tax proposal was put on the May 1984 county ballot to build a $150 million domed stadium. Voters crushed it by a 2 to 1 margin.

But the idea wouldn't die. In 1985, there was a proposal for the Hexatron, a six-sided domed stadium that would be paid for with a sin tax on alcohol and cigarettes. One of the leading proponents was Jeff Jacobs, a young state representative and son of developer Richard Jacobs (a future owner of the Indians). Though the Hexatron never amounted to much more than sketches, momentum continued to grow for some sort of covered stadium.

Cleveland mayor George Voinovich and Ohio governor (and Clevelander) Richard Celeste pushed for the formation of the Greater Cleveland Domed Stadium Corporation to pursue the idea. Cleveland Tomorrow, a group of downtown CEOs, launched a development fund.

The Domed Stadium Corporation in 1985 began acquiring land just south of Tower City for the future site. In the meantime, Cleveland State University announced plans to build its own arena, one that would not only host its basketball team but also compete with a domed stadium for concerts and other events.

The Browns opt out

Modell decided he did not want to share a new facility and its revenues with the Indians and demanded the city offer him a new twenty-year lease on old Municipal Stadium in return for making much-needed improvements. The Indians were bought in 1986 by brothers Richard and David Jacobs, who wanted their team to play in a baseball-only ballpark.

Faced with so many competing interests, the Domed Stadium Corp. abandoned the idea of a complex for all three teams and instead proposed a new baseball-only ballpark and an adjacent arena to bring the Cavs back to the city.

In May 1990, county voters approved a fifteen-year sin tax to build the Gateway Sports and Entertainment Complex. The resulting Jacobs Field and Gund Arena opened in 1994. (Jacobs Field was renamed Progressive Field in 2008, and Gund Arena was renamed

Rocket Mortgage FieldHouse in 2019.) Playing in their new ballpark, the recharged Indians made it to the World Series the following year for the first time since 1954. And the city was again home to an NBA team after twenty years.

The opening of Gateway, while a boon to the Indians, Cavs, and downtown, would have negative repercussions for the city's third pro team. When the Indians moved to Jacobs Field, Modell lost millions in revenue. Already one of the least wealthy NFL owners, Modell was in a financial bind. Now, he demanded that Cleveland build him a new stadium. When the city refused, Modell moved the team to Baltimore. It was the darkest day in the city's sports history.

Cleveland sued to stop the move. In the eventual settlement, Modell surrendered the Browns name and colors, and the city agreed to build a new stadium for a new team. This was another opportunity to build a domed stadium or one with a retractable roof. County Commissioner Lee Weingart argued for a combination domed stadium/convention center to be built near Gateway in order to take advantage of highway access and parking, but Mayor Mike White insisted on an open-air stadium to be built on the same city-owned lakefront site as Municipal Stadium because that would save money and time.

But it also tied up valuable lakefront property for a building that sits idle most of the year.

"It would have been better to have a domed stadium," Weingart said in 2022. "It's hard to have a stadium you can use only eleven days a year. With a domed stadium we would have hosted a Super Bowl by now."

Will there ever be a dome?

The Browns' lease at Cleveland Browns Stadium runs through 2028. At that time, the stadium will be thirty years old, and the team almost certainly will ask for a new one—or significant improvements to the existing one, which could include a retractable roof.

The trend among NFL owners is to demand not only stadiums

but surrounding campuses: hundreds of acres of parking lots and land that can be developed for entertainment, lodging, dining, and offices—all, of course, under the control and for the benefit of the team.

All those amenities come with enormous price tags: Allegiant Stadium, which opened in 2020 as the home of the Las Vegas Raiders, cost $1.9 billion. SoFi Stadium, which also opened in 2020 as home to the Los Angeles Rams and Chargers (also including a park, lake, plaza, concert space, townhomes, and hotel), cost $5.5 billion.

Even if Cleveland could afford something on that scale, it couldn't be built at the current location. FirstEnergy/Cleveland Browns Stadium is hemmed in by the lake and the Port of Cleveland facilities, the Shoreway, railroad tracks, and Burke Lakefront Airport.

Some say the solution is simple: close Burke and convert its 450 acres into a football/entertainment complex. However, it's not that easy. Closing Burke would be difficult, and there almost certainly would be opposition to turning such prime property over to a billionaire team owner.

It has been rumored that the team identified two possible locations for a new stadium with a dome or retractable roof: the site of the Main Post Office southeast of downtown or the area between East 13th and 17th Streets north of St. Clair Avenue.

Of course, it might be easier—though less popular—to build such a complex outside of Cleveland and, possibly, outside Cuyahoga County in a neighboring community. There is precedent. The New England Patriots, Los Angeles Rams, Los Angeles Chargers, New York Giants, New York Jets, San Francisco 49ers, Las Vegas Raiders, Dallas Cowboys, Buffalo Bills, Washington Commanders, Arizona Cardinals, and Miami Dolphins all play in stadiums outside their "home" cities.

Whether area voters and public officials would be willing or able to pay for a new domed or retractable-roof stadium is yet to be determined.

In the meantime, Browns fans will continue to shiver in the December winds off Lake Erie and tell each other that *real* football is played outdoors.

NFL Cities With Fixed or Retractable Roof Stadiums

New Orleans	Phoenix	Los Angeles
Houston	Atlanta	Las Vegas
Detroit	Minneapolis	
Indianapolis	Dallas	

Who Is That Building Named After?

Like many older cities, Cleveland is full of streets, government buildings, parks, and monuments named for prominent (or at least once prominent) local figures, most of them politicians and most of them long gone. Their names live on through their attachment to post offices, schools, and streets, but the men and women behind them—and what they did to deserve the honor—can easily be forgotten.

Here's a rundown of the people behind the names:

Anthony J. Celebrezze Federal Building

The federal office building at the southwest corner of East 9th Street and Lakeside Avenue is named for the forty-ninth mayor of Cleveland (1953–62), who resigned to become Secretary of Health, Education, and Welfare in the Kennedy and Johnson administrations. In 1965 he was appointed federal judge for the 6th Circuit Court of Appeals, serving until 1980 when he retired from active service on the bench. He died in 1998. His son, Anthony J. Celebrezze, Jr., was Ohio attorney general, Ohio secretary of state, and a state senator.

Hope Memorial Bridge

This span over the Cuyahoga River connecting Lorain and Carnegie avenues, formerly the Lorain-Carnegie Bridge, was renamed in 1983 in honor of comedian and actor Bob Hope, whose father, Harry, was a stonemason who helped build the bridge in the 1920s. Bob Hope was born in England, but his family moved to Cleveland when he was five, and it's where he launched his showbiz career.

The bridge is best known for its Guardians of Traffic pylons, which lent their name to Cleveland's baseball team in 2022.

Langston Hughes Branch, Cleveland Public Library

This library branch at East 102nd Street and Superior Avenue is named in honor of the poet, novelist, and activist, who attended high school in Cleveland.

Stephanie Tubbs Jones School, Cleveland Municipal School District, Stephanie Tubbs Jones Hall (Case Western Reserve University, Cleveland Clinic Stephanie Tubbs Jones Health Center

The elementary school (formerly Patrick Henry), residence hall at Case Western Reserve University, and health center in East Cleveland are named in honor of the late congresswoman from the 11th District, who died in office in 2008.

Frank J. Lausche State Office Building

This office tower at the corner of West Superior and Prospect avenues is named in honor of the former Cleveland mayor, two-time Ohio governor, and U.S. senator. Lausche (1895–1990) was known for his integrity and willingness to defy Democratic party bosses.

Fannie M. Lewis Community Park at League Park,
Fannie M. Lewis Community Corrections and Treatment Center

Fannie Lewis was the longest-serving councilwoman in Cleveland history. She represented Ward 7 from 1980–2008 and was a tireless champion for both the Hough neighborhood and civil rights. She also fought for the renovation of historic League Park, which was renamed in her honor in 2013. The Community Corrections and Treatment Center named for her is on East 55th Street.

Howard M. Metzenbaum U.S. Courthouse,
Cuyahoga County Metzenbaum Center,
The Metzenbaum Center

Howard Metzenbaum (1917–2008) was a U.S. senator (Democrat) from Cleveland for nearly twenty years, as well as a businessman and state legislator. He was one of the most liberal members of the Senate and, despite his personal wealth, he advocated for the poor and unions. The Howard M. Metzenbaum U.S. Courthouse on Superior Avenue downtown, formerly the Old Federal Building, was renamed in his honor in 1998. The Metzenbaum Center on Community College Avenue is part of the Cuyahoga County Juvenile Court. The Metzenbaum Center in Chesterland is part of the Geauga County Board of Developmental Disabilities.

Jesse Owens Olympic Oak Plaza,
Jesse C. Owens Post Office

The plaza in University Circle and the post office are named in honor of one of the greatest track-and-field athletes in history. Owens (1913–80), who went to high school in Cleveland, won four gold medals at the Olympics in Berlin in 1936, laying waste to Adolf Hitler's plans to use the games as a platform for Aryan superiority. Owens also has a statue in Fort Huntington Park on West Lakeside Avenue downtown.

Perk Plaza at Chester Commons

This four-block park on East 12th Street is named for Ralph J. Perk, who was the fifty-second mayor of Cleveland. The Republican served from 1971–77 and also was county auditor from 1962–71. He is best remembered for accidentally setting his hair on fire with a welder's torch during a ribbon-cutting ceremony in 1972.

Rockefeller Park, Rockefeller City Greenhouse, Rockefeller Building, Rockefeller Avenue

John D. Rockefeller began a business career in Cleveland that would see him become the wealthiest man in the world thanks to Standard Oil. Though born in Pennsylvania, Rockefeller grew up in Cleveland and started his first company here. He later moved to New York City for business reasons and had a nasty tax dispute with Cleveland, but his generous legacy is still evident.

Carl B. Stokes U.S. Courthouse

The towering courthouse on West Superior Avenue overlooking the Cuyahoga River Valley is named in honor of the first African American elected mayor of a major U.S. city. Stokes (1927–96) was mayor of Cleveland from 1968 to 1972. He later was a TV news anchorman in New York City and U.S. ambassador to the Republic of Seychelles under President Clinton.

Cleveland Public Library Louis Stokes Wing, Louis Stokes Cleveland Veterans Affairs Medical Center, RTA Louis Stokes Station at Windermere

Louis Stokes, brother of Carl, was an attorney, civil rights pioneer, and the first African American congressman elected in Ohio. Stokes (1925–2015) served fifteen terms in Congress, was chairman of the House Intelligence Committee, and head of the Congressional Black Caucus.

Voinovich Bicentennial Park,
George V. Voinovich Bridges,
George Voinovich High School, Cleveland Municipal School District

George Voinovich (1936–2016) was a Cleveland mayor, Ohio governor, and U.S. senator. He is best-known for leading the city's comeback in the 1980s. In the Senate, he was a moderate Republican who could work with Democrats, a skill he developed in Cleveland. The park is part of North Coast Harbor at the end of East 9th Street. and the bridges carry the Innerbelt section of I-90 over the Cuyahoga River Valley.

Why Is Blossom Music Center Traffic So Awful?

Blossom Music Center is a treasure, one of the most beautiful outdoor music venues in the country. Tucked away inside the Cuyahoga Valley, thirty miles south of Cleveland, it is serene, secluded—and an absolute nightmare to get in and out of.

Everyone who's been there, whether to see Kenny Chesney or The Black Keys, has a horror story about missing an opening act while stuck on Steels Corners Road, and then idling for hours after the show while waiting for the parking lot to clear. Most of us chalk it up as part of the price to pay for seeing a show at Blossom. But not everyone.

In 2021, an attorney who said she missed the Jackson Browne portion of a twin bill with James Taylor filed a complaint with the Ohio Attorney General's Office of Consumer Protection seeking a refund for herself and "thousands of others" due to "inaccessibility to the venue."

Blossom Music Center is owned by the Musical Arts Association, the parent organization of the Cleveland Orchestra, but the pop, rock, and country shows are promoted and managed by Live Nation. An orchestra spokeswoman referred questions about traffic to Live Nation, which did not respond to requests for comment.

No one is more familiar with Blossom traffic than the Summit County Sheriff's Department, which directs traffic on concert nights. The roads surrounding Blossom simply weren't built to handle a music venue that can accommodate 23,000, said Inspector Bill Holland. The inevitable fender benders, breakdowns, and road construction can also cause delays.

In 2018, Cuyahoga Falls, the city in which Blossom is located, offered resident-access passes to those who live close to the venue in order for them to get preferential treatment through the traffic on concert nights.

Why not just widen the roads so more traffic can flow through? Residents and businesses don't want to surrender their yards to make life easier for concertgoers, let alone pay for the construction, Holland said.

The other obstacle is Cuyahoga Valley National Park, which surrounds Blossom and is largely off limits for new road building.

Of course, getting onto the Blossom grounds doesn't end the traffic jams. Parking in the lots and on surrounding fields can be chaotic, and the wait to exit can be as long as the concert itself. At night's end, sheriff's deputies also must deal with stragglers who can't find their cars or who have been left stranded by their drivers.

Traffic is generally lighter for Cleveland Orchestra concerts than for other shows, but even those have been known to tie things up.

What will ever be done to solve the problem? Probably nothing, Holland said. Despite the traffic jams, concertgoers still find the trip worthwhile.

Why Is Ohio State Football So Popular in Cleveland?

It's a Saturday afternoon in the fall, and porches everywhere are draped with scarlet-and-gray flags. It seems as if every TV is tuned to the Ohio State Buckeyes game. Sports bars are crowded with people wearing Buckeyes shirts and hats. The outcome of that day's game will be covered in depth in the local paper and on TV news.

But those porches and sports bars aren't in Columbus, home of Ohio State University; they're in Cleveland, 140 miles away. As college football fan loyalties go, Cleveland might as well be Columbus North.

There are other Division I football programs closer to Cleveland—Kent State University, the University of Akron, and Youngstown State University—but they don't have nearly the same following as the Buckeyes.

Here's why Cleveland bleeds scarlet and gray.

There's no one else to root for

Local fans of top-level college football have to look elsewhere. Cleveland State University doesn't have a football program. Case Western Reserve University, John Carroll University, Oberlin College, Hiram College, and Baldwin Wallace University are all Division III programs.

If any conference ought to have a claim on Ohio, it should be the Mid-American Conference (MAC), six of whose twelve schools are in the state: The University of Akron, Bowling Green State University, Kent State, Miami University, Ohio University, and University of Toledo. But MAC football is a level below the Power 5 conferences like the Big 10, and while it's not unusual for the best MAC schools to wind up in minor bowl games, they've never been in the College Football Playoff.

Only the University of Cincinnati in the American Athletic Conference, the successor to the Big East, occasionally comes within a Hail Mary of Ohio State's level.

Ohio State is the only Power 5 Conference team in the state and the only school to consistently be in the national championship hunt.

Everyone loves a winner

Ohio State is consistently one of the best programs in the country. It has won eight national titles and forty-one conference titles, and it has been in the College Football Playoff five times. Consistent winning brings popularity and ensures fans remain true.

Cleveland doesn't have a natural rivalry with Columbus that would dilute the fan devotion. Unlike Cincinnati, whose Bengals compete with the Cleveland Browns, Columbus has only one professional sports team: the NHL Blue Jackets. And Cleveland does not have an NHL team.

There are a lot of Buckeyes in Cleveland

Tens of thousands of Ohio State alumni live in Northeast Ohio. It's only natural that they keep their allegiance to their alma mater.

Northeast Ohio high schools have been consistent suppliers of talent for the Buckeyes, particularly Glenville under longtime coach Ted Ginn, Sr., whose own son played for Ohio State. From 2002 to 2014, for example, the Buckeyes recruited at least one player per year from Glenville, for a total of twenty-two.

Of course, the legions of alumni and local players can't account for the entire fan base. Take Mark Rogozinski. The fifty-year-old Mayfield Heights resident grew up in Greater Cleveland and graduated from Cleveland State. He's never lived in Columbus, but he watches every Buckeyes game on TV and even tapes them for rewatching. He follows recruiting classes and is a regular on fan forums.

The obsession began in college when he visited buddies at Ohio State. "For me, it was going to games with friends and that whole collegiate atmosphere," he said.

He and his friends would reunite annually at OSU games, but he stopped attending when his son was born. The group now watches games on TV together. Mark took his son to his first game in the 2022 season.

"I'm more of a Buckeyes fan than a Browns fan. I just like the college game better," he said.

True, you might see the occasional Michigan or Penn State flag on a porch on Saturdays in the fall, but there is no doubt that Northeast Ohio is Buckeyes territory.

How Come All Those Museums Are In One Spot— University Circle?

University Circle, roughly one square mile in area, is one of the densest concentrations of cultural, medical, and educational institutions in the world. The neighborhood is second in Northeast Ohio only to downtown Cleveland in number of jobs and in the visitors it attracts for concerts, art exhibits, and more.

Its boundaries are Wade Park Avenue on the north, East 105th Street on the west, and RTA tracks to the south and east. The adjacent neighborhood of Little Italy is generally considered to be outside of University Circle.

A town built around a tavern

The neighborhood that became home to so many world-class museums and institutions got its start with a . . . tavern.

Blacksmith Nathaniel Doan was part of the Connecticut Land Company's first two surveying expeditions to the Western Reserve in 1796 and 1797. In 1799, he built a hotel and tavern at what is now the northwest corner of Euclid Avenue and East 107th Street. Doan's Tavern remained in business for fifty years, and the community of Doan's Corners grew up around it.

The "University" connection came when Western Reserve University relocated from Hudson, Ohio, to Adelbert Road in 1883. In 1885, Case School of Applied Science became its neighbor, moving from downtown. The neighboring schools would merge in 1967 to form Case Western Reserve University (CWRU).

The "Circle" referred to an 1880s streetcar turnaround at Euclid and Doan Brook Boulevard (later Liberty Boulevard and then

Several of University Circle's many arts institutions surround Wade Lagoon.
Becky Voldrich, University Circle Inc.

renamed Martin Luther King, Jr. Boulevard in 1981).

The emergence of a cultural hub didn't result from city planning but is owed to the generosity and vision of the city's leading citizens and philanthropists.

Industrialist Jeptha Wade in 1882 donated sixty-three acres of land to the city that became home first to the Wade Park Zoo and later the Cleveland Botanical Garden. Other institutions followed: Western Reserve Historical Society (1898), Cleveland Museum of Natural History (1920), Cleveland Museum of Art (1913), and University Hospitals and Severance Hall (both in 1931).

After World War II, nearly all the wealthy residents in the Wade Park neighborhood had moved to the suburbs, some leaving behind luxury residences that the growing cultural institutions either demolished or converted to their own uses.

Saving the Circle

In 1957, civic leaders and the city created the University Circle Development Foundation and adopted a master plan that called for the institutions to remain in the Circle, embrace a common vision, and cooperate in its realization. For years its primary mission was as a land bank, securing undeveloped, underdeveloped, and declining property to allow CWRU, University Hospitals, and others to expand. It also took on the responsibility of comprehensive planning for parking, transportation, safety, and other issues.

The foundation was reorganized in 1970 as University Circle, Inc. (UCI), with the mission to better connect the Circle and its offerings to the neighborhoods around it. The Hough riots and Glenville shootout in the late 1960s made apparent the divide between the predominantly White and suburban-focused Circle institutions and the neighboring majority-Black residential communities of Glenville, Hough, Fairfax, and East Cleveland.

UCI has been more successful in a second mission: making the Circle a residential neighborhood again. Throughout its history, University Circle has always had more visitors than residents; most of the people living in the neighborhood were students.

Since 2010, UCI has worked to create a permanent population base with the necessary amenities. Development of the Uptown District added retail, restaurants, and residences along Euclid between Mayfield Road and East 115th Street. Thousands of apartments have been added or are being planned.

In 2020, approximately 30,000 people worked in University Circle and 9,000 lived there, a nearly 90 percent increase in 10 years.

University Circle Institutions

Museums

Cleveland Museum of Art

Museum of Contemporary Art Cleveland

Western Reserve Historical Society/ Cleveland History Center

Cleveland Museum of Natural History

Dunham Tavern Museum

Dittrick Medical History Center and Museum

Educational

Case Western Reserve University

The Music Settlement

Cleveland Institute of Art

Cleveland Institute of Music

Center for Arts-Inspired Learning

Institute for Creative Leadership

Cultural

Cleveland Botanical Garden

Cleveland Cinematheque

Cleveland Orchestra

Karamu House

The Sculpture Center

Cleveland Piano (Cleveland International Piano Competition)

Artists Archives of the Western Reserve

Cleveland Cultural Gardens

Social Service

Magnolia Clubhouse

Ronald McDonald House Charities of Northeast Ohio

United Cerebral Palsy of Greater Cleveland

Transplant House of Cleveland

Mt. Sinai Health Care Foundation

Medical

University Hospitals

Louis Stokes Cleveland Veterans Affairs Medical Center

Cleveland Hearing & Speech Center

Cleveland Sight Center

Centers for Dialysis Care

Parks

Wade Oval

Nord Family Greenway

Rockefeller Park

Ambler Park

Fine Arts Garden (Wade Lagoon)

Tony Brush Park

Historic Landmarks

Cozad-Bates House

Hessler Historic District

East Cleveland Township Cemetery

Lake View Cemetery

Hart Crane Memorial

How Did Little Italy Survive?

Cleveland's Little Italy neighborhood is one of the most distinctive and sharply defined in the city. No one driving along Mayfield Road between University Circle and Cleveland Heights could fail to realize that they're passing through an ethnic enclave with its own history, identity, and culture.

While Little Italy (or Murray Hill, as it's sometimes known) has changed over the decades, it has retained its identity better than most of the city's ethnic strongholds. It outlasted Cleveland's four other Italian neighborhoods, including "Big Italy" in the Woodland Avenue/Central Market neighborhood.

There are other Italian pockets in the city, including the parishes of St. Rocco's, Holy Redeemer, and Mt. Carmel, but Murray Hill has done the best in keeping its numbers and identity.

It's ironic that such a lively neighborhood owes its existence to a cemetery.

In 1880, Giuseppe Carabelli, an Italian immigrant and sculptor, moved from New York City to Cleveland. He founded Lakeview Granite & Monumental Works, which sculpted many of the monuments at neighboring Lake View Cemetery. The company's success drew other Italian immigrants, primarily from the Campobasso province, who settled along Mayfield Road.

The men helped build the city's bridges, sewers, and streetcars, while the women worked in the clothing and garment industries. The villagers brought their Catholic faith with them, and the Scalabrini Fathers from Italy followed the immigrants to the rapidly growing neighborhood. Holy Rosary Parish was commissioned by the Cleveland Catholic Diocese in 1891 and still serves as the community's spiritual anchor.

The annual Feast of the Assumption packs Little Italy. The neighborhood got its start thanks to a cemetery. *Erik Drost, via Flickr / CC BY 2.0*

A few blocks away on Mayfield Road is Alta House. Built in 1900 by John D. Rockefeller as a settlement house for Italian immigrants and named after his daughter, Alta House provided a variety of services, including a daycare and classes.

Alta House still serves the neighborhood, but the original structure was torn down and a new building erected in its place.

And pasta lovers everywhere owe a debt to Little Italy immigrant Angelo Vitantonio, who invented the hand-cranked pasta machine in 1906. The company he founded, VillaWare, is still in existence.

Fight for survival

Despite its strong traditions, in the 1970s Little Italy nearly went the path of so many other ethnic enclaves, said Pamela Dean, head of the Italian American Museum of Cleveland, which is located next to Presti's Bakery. Families were moving out as neighboring University Hospitals and Case Western Reserve University encroached.

"There was a core group that fought to keep it intact and that really cares about community," Dean said.

This group formed the Mayfield–Murray Hill District Council, which got the city to grant the neighborhood historic status, thus offering some protection against deterioration.

The neighborhood long had a reputation as being insular and hostile to outsiders, particularly Blacks. Even as the hospital, University Circle, and Case Western pushed against its borders, Little Italy resisted encroachment and diversification.

But in the past few decades, Little Italy has welcomed a more diverse group, including CWRU students. (In some cases, families moved out of the neighborhood but kept the family house and rented it to students.) Art galleries and boutiques have joined the the shops and restaurants that make the neighborhood such a draw. And the annual Feast of the Assumption still draws thousands every summer to one of Northeast Ohio's most vibrant communities.

However, for some, the battle to preserve Little Italy continues. Multifamily housing has brought new residents but threatens the neighborhood's identity. Dean said she fears the community is nearing a tipping point of new development that could permanently harm its nature.

"There has to be a balance," she said.

Why Did John D. Rockefeller Leave Cleveland?

The final resting place of one of the richest men in the world is on top of a hill in East Cleveland.

John D. Rockefeller rests under a tall white obelisk, surrounded by the graves of family, in Lake View Cemetery.

That Rockefeller chose to be buried in the commmunity that launched him on his way to building an unimaginable fortune, then sued him, then lost him, speaks to the tycoon's complicated relationship with the city.

Rockefeller wasn't a native son. He was born on a farm in 1839 near Richard, New York. The family moved to Strongsville, Ohio, in 1853 and the young man attended Central High School in Cleveland. In 1855, with a few business college courses under his belt, he became an assistant bookkeeper for a Cleveland firm that bought, sold, and shipped grain, coal, and other commodities. Four years later, he and a partner started their own business, which prospered during the Civil War.

In 1863, Rockefeller entered the nascent oil business, which was disorganized and divided among small operators. He began acquiring small drillers and refiners, then added more and more until in 1870 he created Standard Oil, a company that would dominate oil refining and distribution for decades until it was broken up in 1911 by a government antitrust lawsuit.

As Standard Oil grew, Rockefeller began spending more time in New York City, the country's financial capital. He eventually moved Standard Oil headquarters there in 1885. However, he still kept two homes in Cleveland, the house on Euclid Avenue's Millionaires' Row and a summer place at Forest Hill, the then-rural

John D. Rockefeller left Cleveland at the height of his business success, but he came back—after he died. Forest Hill Park, site of his former estate, is just part of his legacy here. *Library of Congress*

estate in what is now Cleveland Heights and East Cleveland.

A relationship gone sour

As Rockefeller's business shifted away from Cleveland, so did his tax dollars, a loss that upset local officials. The oilman was careful to keep his summer stays in Cleveland short enough to avoid incurring local tax liabilities. However, in 1912, his wife, Cettie, fell ill and the couple was forced to remain in town.

Once the stay extended past the February 1, 1913, deadline, the county presented him with a $1.5 million tax bill. Rockefeller refused to pay. At one point, he was banned from entering Ohio. The courts eventually ruled in his favor, but the dispute soured Rockefeller on Cleveland—to a degree.

Luckily for the city, the World's Richest Man continued to donate to local charities and organizations, including the Western Reserve Historical Society, YMCA, Early Settlers Association, and Erie Street Baptist Church (later Euclid Avenue Baptist Church). Other beneficiaries were Bethel Union, the Visiting Nurse Association of Cleveland, Children's Fresh Air Camp, the Woman's Christian Temperance Union, and Alta House in Little Italy.

While he did not return to Cleveland for the last two decades of his life, the estrangement did not affect his plans for eternity.

A rich legacy

Rockefeller died at age ninety-eight in 1937 at his home in Ormond Beach, Florida. Like everything else in his life, Rockefeller's burial was meticulously planned. Sometime before 1882, well before the tax dispute, he had bought a 17,000-square-foot family plot on one of the highest points in Lake View Cemetery, where he had once been a trustee. He had even commissioned his own monument, a 70-foot-high Egyptian obelisk that was carved in four pieces in a granite quarry in Vermont, then shipped to Cleveland and installed on the hilltop by a stonecutting firm in nearby Little Italy in 1899, thirty-eight years before Rockefeller's death.

The Rockefeller legacy in Cleveland is extensive. It includes the Rockefeller Building at West 6th Street and Superior Avenue, where the tycoon had offices; Forest Hill Park; and Rockefeller Park, for which he donated land.

Though Standard Oil eventually moved out of Cleveland, it was partly responsible for the creation of an industrial base that would power the city's growth. Businesses that relied on oil or helped manufacture it moved to Cleveland for proximity to the oil giant. For example, Sherwin-Williams opened its first paint factory in a former Standard Oil cooperage. The paint company that would become Glidden started here in 1875. Rockefeller and Standard Oil set Cleveland on its path to industrial might.

Standard Oil moving its headquarters to New York City might have been inevitable, but without the tax dispute, Rockefeller might have continued to be a part-time resident of Cleveland. Had that been the case, it's likely his philanthropic legacy here would have been even greater.

Why Is the Coventry Neighborhood the Hippie Heart of Cleveland?

Though now a shadow of its former counterculture self, Coventry Village was once the closest thing Greater Cleveland had to Greenwich Village or Haight-Ashbury.

In the latter half of the 1960s and '70s, Coventry Road between Mayfield Road and Euclid Heights Boulevard in Cleveland Heights was home to a vibrant mix of hippies, Jewish mom-and-pop stores, slumming college students, biker gangs, artists, and others who just didn't fit in elsewhere.

The street became a destination for high school kids and young adults who wanted a taste of the counterculture lifestyle without actually having to move to New York or San Francisco.

The best-laid plans

Ironically, Coventry was originally intended to be an exclusive neighborhood for the well-to-do—the exact opposite of what it became.

In the 1890s, the planned community of Euclid Heights was to be a haven for members of Cleveland's upper crust, who were moving east out of Cleveland to escape the city's growth. However, in the 1910s, the failure of the property development company led to the breakup of some large estates and the construction instead of a number of apartment buildings that offered affordable housing.

That opened the door to a mix of residents, including immigrants and small merchants. In the 1920s, the neighborhood became a haven for Jews moving from the neighborhoods of Glenville and Hough. They opened businesses along Coventry Road to serve commuters using a streetcar hub at the intersection with Mayfield Road.

Coventry changed again in the last half of the 1960s when Cleveland's youth counterculture made it its own. Many Jewish residents moved farther east, and their shops were replaced by record stores, head shops, and clothing boutiques. Bikers also found it to be friendly territory and turned bars into hangouts.

The Heights Theater

The neighborhood's bohemian nature is reflected in the history of the Heights Theater, which opened in 1919 on Euclid Heights Boulevard. In 1922, the movie house was raided for showing a movie on a Sunday afternoon, a violation of community "blue laws."

In 1954, the theater was renamed the Heights Art Theater with a mission to show international films, becoming the city's first art house. That choice of fare got the theater into trouble in 1959 when it screened Louis Malle's *Les Amant*s (The Lovers). The film was controversial for its depiction of a love triangle involving a married woman and for a brief glimpse of a female breast.

Cleveland Heights police raided the theater, confiscated the film, and arrested manager Nico Jacobellis, who was found guilty of possessing and showing an obscene film. His attorneys appealed the case all the way to the U.S. Supreme Court, which in 1964 reversed the lower court's decision in a landmark ruling that declared the movie was not obscene and was therefore constitutionally protected.

The ruling is best remembered for Justice Potter Stewart's opinion that, when it comes to obscene material, "I know it when I see it."

Ironically, in the 1970s and 1980s, the Heights Art Theater switched to showing actual pornographic films. It was also known for midnight showings of *The Rocky Horror Picture Show*. In 1984 it changed its name to the Coventry Theater, then to the Centrum, screening mainstream fare. It closed as a theater in 2003, and the space is now a church.

Two mainstays of Coventry Road in Cleveland Heights. *Jim Sweeney*

Eccentric and proud

Though the neighborhood is no longer the alternative hub it was, there are still remnants of its tie-dyed past.

Perhaps no business is as identified with Coventry as Tommy's, which opened as one of Cleveland's first vegetarian restaurant in 1972. A fire and rent hikes have it on its fourth location on the street, but owner Tommy Fello said he never considered leaving: "We never wanted to be anywhere else, and thank God we're still here today."

A small park at the corner of Coventry and Euclid Heights is named for the late graphic novelist Harvey Pekar, the subject of the 2003 film *American Splendor*. The neighborhood was a favorite hangout for Pekar, who browsed for old jazz records at shops along the street and argued politics at Tommy's.

Coventry has largely resisted chain stores and is still home to perhaps the largest concentration of independent businesses in Northeast Ohio, some of which have been around for more than fifty years.

Mac's Backs—Books on Coventry opened in 1982 and is on its third location on the street. Owner Suzanne DeGaetano, who's been there the entire time, said there is nowhere she'd rather be.

"I think it's one of the best places to do business in Northeast Ohio," she said, adding that the family-friendly vibe, affordability, small scale of the buildings, and welcoming atmosphere make it a community touchstone.

"It's a crossroads. It's a melting pot, and its strength has always been its diversity," DeGaetano said. "People are looking for an experience. That's what indies provide."

In 2023, Coventry lost one of its anchors — Record Revolution, which closed after fifty-five years. Despite all the businesses that have come and gone, the alternative essence of Coventry has remained the same.

"It's a mindset down here," Tommy Fello said.

Coventry Village institutions

Mac's Backs—Books on Coventry

Passport to Peru

Tommy's Restaurant

Inn on Coventry

Heights Hardware

Grog Shop

Attenson's Antiques & Books

The Exchange

Sunshine Headquarters Too

East Side or West Side?
(And Does It Still Matter?)

Newcomers to Greater Cleveland are often puzzled by the empha-
sis locals place on the divide between the East Side and West
Side and their insistence on identifying with one side or the other.
Cleveland is a relatively compact city, after all, and it's possible to
drive from one end of Cuyahoga County to the other in an hour, so
why the rift? Inform those newcomers that East Siders and West
Siders once fought an armed battle over a Cuyahoga River bridge,
and they'll be absolutely baffled.

At its beginning, Cleveland did not have two sides. General
Moses Cleaveland founded the city on the east bank of the
Cuyahoga River, and its first years of growth were on that side.

In choosing the east bank, Cleaveland was following the terms
of the Treaty of Fort McIntosh, negotiated in 1785 between the
American government and four Native American tribes. It set the
westernmost limit of U.S. dominion at the Cuyahoga River: the
United States (and civilization) to the east, Native Americans (and
wilderness) to the west.

That treaty was, of course, eventually violated by settlers, who
settled on the west side of the Cuyahoga, forming a separate town.

The Battle of the Bridge

Ohio City, or City of Ohio, as it was known, was founded on the
west bank of the Cuyahoga in 1818 as part of Brooklyn Township.
It incorporated in March 1836, actually beating Cleveland's incor-
poration by two days.

Facing off on opposite banks, the two cities were fierce economic rivals, particularly in the areas of shipbuilding and canal
boat traffic. Their rivalry came to a head in April 1836 when Cleve-

land opened the new Columbus Road Bridge, the first permanent span over the Cuyahoga. Previously, travelers between the two cities had used a floating bridge at Center Street, a span jointly owned by the two municipalities.

The new bridge allowed traffic from the south to bypass Ohio City's business district and proceed straight into Cleveland. Ohio City merchants correctly viewed it as a direct threat to their economic future, so they boycotted it. In retaliation for the boycott, Cleveland, in June 1836, removed its half of the floating Center Street Bridge, forcing all traffic onto the new Columbus Road span.

Taking up the battle cry, "Two Bridges or None!", Ohio City residents tried unsuccessfully to blow up the Columbus Road Bridge and dug ditches at either end to stop traffic. On October 31, 1836, a mob of armed Ohio City residents set out to demolish the span. They were met by an East Side militia led by the Cleveland mayor. Shots were fired. Three men were seriously wounded before the sheriff broke up the battle.

The fight then moved to the local courts, which issued an injunction preventing further interference with the Columbus Road Bridge. And it also ruled that there should be more than one span.

Eventually, Ohio City could no longer compete economically with its larger neighbor, and it was annexed by Cleveland in 1854.

Perhaps because of its original independence, Ohio City has retained its identity and is now one of the city's most distinctive neighborhoods.

East-West stereotypes

No one is battling over bridges anymore, yet the psychological East-West divide remains, though greatly diminished.

As in every "us versus them" scenario, stereotypes abound:

East Siders are rich, sophisticated, WASP-y and snooty; West Siders are hard-working, salt-of-the-earth, ethnic types.

White collar to the East; blue collar to the West.

East Siders golf; West Siders bowl.

East Siders drive BMWs; West Siders favor Fords and Chevys.

East Siders dine at bistros; West Siders eat at Olive Garden.

East Siders belong to country clubs; West Siders belong to softball leagues.

You get the picture.

East Side/West Side also has become shorthand for the city's racial divide: Blacks on the East side and (mostly ethnic) Whites on the West.

While there are people who swear allegiance to one side of town and travel to the other only out of necessity, the rivalry is fading. It wasn't uncommon up until the 1980s for people to live almost exclusively on their side of town, seldom crossing the river, at least of their own volition.

News commentator Dick Feagler once said, "When I lived on the East Side as a boy, the only thing I knew about the West Side was that the sun set somewhere over there. It might as well have been Alaska."

Also, the growth of the downtown population has created a third class of citizen, one that doesn't pay any attention to the rivalry. While the West Side technically starts just west of Public Square, most people regard the Cuyahoga River as the dividing line. However, residents regard downtown as neutral ground.

The East Side versus West Side debate will continue to be a thing, partly because of racial coding, but also because it's fun.

The late *Plain Dealer* columnist Michael Heaton once summed it up this way:

> So maybe this east-west division is just as it ought to be. Maybe we should simply celebrate the difference instead of continually asking why it's there. Instead of asking why the glass is divided in half, why can't we be glad that there are two sides to drink from? We've got two cities in one here. And despite what people tell you, you don't need a passport to cross the Cuyahoga. All that's required is an open mind and a sense of adventure.

Why Doesn't CSU Have a Football Team?

Cleveland is a football-mad town in a football-mad state. Its unwavering loyalty to the Browns and Ohio State Buckeyes is proof of that.

But its hometown public university doesn't have a football team. Never has and probably never will. Of the fourteen public universities in Ohio, Cleveland State University is one of only three that doesn't have a team. And the other two are a medical school and a glorified community college.

Established as a state university in 1964, Cleveland State University adopted the buildings, faculty, staff, and curriculum of Fenn College, a private school. Unlike other large public universities, such as Kent State, Bowling Green, and Miami, CSU was for most of its first five decades primarily a commuter university. Located downtown, it didn't have space for a stadium nor a residential fan base of students. There simply wasn't interest in a football team.

However, starting in the early 2000s, the school began trying to create more of a campus feel, adding student housing and amenities. In 2008, CSU president Michael Schwartz floated the idea of starting a team to enhance the college experience and give the school more of a campus feel. The idea was to join the Football Championship Subdivision (formerly Division I-AA) and compete in the Pioneer Football League against such schools as Butler and Dayton.

A consultant estimated football would cost $13 million to $15 million to launch and roughly $1 million a year to operate. CSU also would need a home field and practice facilities, which would come at an additional cost.

In 2010 the student government polled students on whether

they would be interested in adding a Division I nonscholarship team and how much they'd be willing to pay to cover the costs. Sixty-nine percent of students said they wanted a team, but 56 percent said they were opposed to paying an additional fee.

"I don't consider it an overwhelming mandate," CSU president Ron Berkman told *cleveland.com* at the time.

The idea hasn't gained any momentum since.

How Did AsiaTown Get to Be Where It Is?

Walk the streets of AsiaTown and it's easy to assume that it's been there forever. The community just east of downtown, between the Innerbelt and East 40th Street, Perkins to St. Clair Avenues, has the feel of a neighborhood that has seen the city grow up around it.

In fact, Cleveland's first Chinatown in 1860 was centered on what is now West 3rd Street, just west of Ontario Street. It was settled largely by Chinese immigrants who had relocated from the West Coast to escape racism and discrimination.

By the 1920s, downtown growth had pushed the community eastward to Rockwell Avenue between East 21st and 24th Streets. Rockwell became a lively strip of Chinese restaurants and shops, some of which survive today in the area known as Old Chinatown. Restaurants like the Red Dragon Cafe and Golden Gate drew White patrons eager to try exotic dishes like chow mein and egg rolls.

Two merchant associations, On Leong Tong and Hip Sing, were formed to support the community and preserve its values. Chinatown spread eastward to East 40th Street as its population grew, particularly after the Communist takeover of China in 1949 led to an influx of immigrants.

However, Chinatown fell into a decline in the 1970s as some residents moved to the suburbs and were replaced by non-Chinese. The formerly tight-knit community began to lose its cohesion. Ironically, Chinatown was saved by other Asians. Korean and Vietnamese immigrants began moving into the neighborhood in the 1980s, bringing more residents and a new diversity. The changing ethnic makeup led to changing the name from Chinatown to AsiaTown in 2007.

"It survives because it's an immigrant community," said Lisa Wong, an unofficial ambassador for the neighborhood. It's the largest Asian neighborhood in Northeast Ohio and draws people from around the state and western Pennsylvania, she said, adding that shopping and eating in AsiaTown is a way for Asian Americans to remain connected to their roots.

The neighborhood is changing, however, with more Black residents and various Cleveland State student renters. It's represented on City Council by Ward 7 councilwoman Stephanie Howse, who would like to see AsiaTown become less insular. Her vision for the ward is to create a communal space where all the residents can mingle and become better acquainted.

"As Clevelanders, we don't mix very well," she said. "Just because you live next to someone doesn't make you neighbors."

While AsiaTown might be more insular than some city neighborhoods, Asia Plaza on Payne Avenue and the annual Asian Festival attract tens of thousands of visitors from throughout the region, exposing them to the community's charms.

Where Do Those 'CHOC' Stickers Come From and What Do They Mean?

Oval, striped "CHOC" stickers are as common on Cleveland bumpers as rust and dings, but where do they come from?

They're a long-running advertisement for Malley's Chocolates, the candy company founded in Lakewood in 1935. Malley's has been distributing the distinctive stickers since 2007, and fans have been slapping them on their cars, golf carts, boats, refrigerators, and Rascal scooters ever since.

They're the brainchild of Dan Malley, former vice president of marketing for the family firm. He got the idea during a trip to Germany, where he saw cars with oval Euro stickers advertising their countries of origin through abbreviations like ITA and GB. He didn't want to be so obvious as to put the company name on the sticker, so he chose the intriguing CHOC for chocolate. The trademark brown, green, and pink coloring helped with identification.

The company has distributed more than 100,000 stickers, and they adorn bumpers in every state and multiple countries. They've even become a way for Greater Clevelanders to spot each other far from home. Malley said he heard of two out-of-state couples who met after spotting each other's stickers in a parking lot and who still reunite once a year in the same lot.

Of course, the spread of the stickers has been helped by Malley's long-running contest, which awards a $25 gift certificate daily to a registered owner whose car is spotted in the wild by Dan Malley or another employee. Those winners are then entered in a monthly drawing to win a $500 gift certificate.

"It really cuts across all demographics. We've seen the stickers on cars driven by sixteen-year-olds to ninety-year-olds," Malley said, adding that he's seen pictures of the stickers on military vehicles in Iraq and on house shutters flanking a bay window.

Malley is also responsible for one of the most distinctive ads in the entire state: the three pink silos along I-480 at the company factory on Brookpark Road in Brook Park.

He wanted to put up a billboard, but the Highway Beautification Act limited the placement of signs near an interstate. The law didn't say anything about silos, however.

When a plastic factory on the other side of I-480 closed in 2011, Malley had a brainstorm. He bought six of the empty silos from the factory, moved them to Malley's property, stacked them to make three eighty-eight-foot silos, painted them Malley's pink, and labeled them Milk, Cocoa, and Sugar.

The result? A non-billboard billboard that is the most recognizable sign in Greater Cleveland. "It's a way of saying Malley's without saying Malley's," he said.

People regularly pull into the lot to have their picture taken in front of the silos. And, yes, some of them think the units are filled with the labeled ingredients (they're empty!). Locals flying into nearby Cleveland Hopkins International Airport know they're home when they spot the silos from the window seats.

"They're a better sign than any billboard could be," Malley said. "They're landmarks."

What the Heck Is "Free Stamp"?

It scarcely merits a second glance now, but *Free Stamp*, the pop art sculpture at East 9th Street and Lakeside Avenue, was once the most controversial piece of public art in the city.

The sculpture was commissioned in 1985 by Standard Oil of Ohio (Sohio) to distinguish its new headquarters on Public Square. The sculptors were husband-and-wife team Claes Oldenburg and Coosje van Bruggen, who were famous for oversized renditions of everyday objects, like a toothpaste tube and a vacuum cleaner.

The bright red *Free Stamp* is typical of their style. Built of aluminum and steel, it's 49 feet long, 28 feet high, and weighs 35 tons. Its location, though, is not where they planned. In 1986, Sohio had been sold to British Petroleum America (BP), and the new owners refused to allow installation of the sculpture in front of their towering new headquarters.

Art historian Edward J. Olszewski, who later wrote a book about *Free Stamp*, speculated that the British suspected the sculpture was an anticorporate commentary. Olszewski noted that pop art is viewed more cynically in Europe than in the United States, where it tends to be seen as whimsical.

To rid itself of the sculpture, BP donated it to the city.

According to Oldenburg, the *Free Stamp* message had nothing to do with its corporate sponsors but was a commentary on the freeing of slaves. Its intended location was across from the Soldiers' & Sailors' Monument, which commemorates the Civil War.

Homeless and unwanted, *Free Stamp* was stored in an Illinois warehouse for five years. Cleveland mayor Mike White then invited the sculptors to Cleveland to find their work a new home.

It wasn't supposed to be here. *Curtis Albert, via Flickr / CC BY 2.0*

That would turn out to be Willard Park, though the controversy wasn't quite over.

The original plan was for *Free Stamp* to stand upright, with the lettering on the stamp's face not visible. However, the city wanted it on its side with the word "FREE" clearly visible. That view prevailed, and the sculpture was installed in 1991. It has been noted that it points at its originally intended home, the former BP Building (later renamed 200 Public Square).

Ironically, though the controversy over the statue itself has long since faded, *Free Stamp*, because of its proximity to City Hall, still finds itself at the center of demonstrations, during which it is sometimes scaled by protestors and hung with banners. And during the 2016 celebration of the Cavaliers championship, fans found the sculpture to be a great vantage point for the victory parade.

Those who want to see more of Claes Oldenburg's work can find two sculptures at the Cleveland Museum of Art: *Standing Mitt with Ball* and *Giant Toothpaste Tube*. In addition, Oberlin College's Allen Memorial Art Museum has *Giant Three-Way Plug*, and the Akron Art Museum is home to *Inverted Q*, an alphabet soup letter.

How Did Cleveland's Latin American Community Become Centered On the Near West Side?

Cleveland's growing Latino population is centered primarily on the city's near West Side, from West 5th to West 65th Streets between Detroit and Clark Avenues.

But, as has been the case over the years with Jewish, Asian, Irish, Black, and other communities, the Latino community's center has shifted over the decades and continues to change.

The first Latinos in Cleveland were Mexicans who arrived in the 1920s, many fleeing the Mexican Revolution. While many came first to work in steel mills in Lorain, a sizable number moved eastward to Cleveland to work in mills, factories, and heavy industry.

Most lived on the near East Side near the present-day main campus of Cuyahoga Community College. In 1932, the community formed Club Azteca as a forum and to preserve its heritage, with members taking turns hosting meetings. It found a permanent home in 1957 in the 5600 block of Detroit Avenue, at the center of the community.

Puerto Ricans were the second Latino group to arrive in numbers. They were recruited in the 1950s to work in the steel mills and other factories. They settled primarily on the East Side around Hough, Lexington, and Superior, close to Our Lady of Fatima Catholic Church and St. Paul's Church, which had Spanish-speaking priests.

The population largely migrated to the near West Side in the late 1950s and early 1960s. In 1975, the Cleveland Catholic Diocese created San Juan Batista on West 54th Street, the first parish specifically for the Latino community.

While Puerto Rican and Mexican are the city's two largest Latino nationalities, Cleveland also has attracted Cubans, Guatemalans, Salvadorans, Venezuelans, Colombians, Dominicans, Peruvians, and others.

Growing numbers

Even as the city has lost residents, the Latino population is growing. According to the 2020 Census, Cleveland gained more than 9,000 Latinos to increase the total number to about 40,000, or 13 percent of the population.

Within Cleveland, the Clark-Fulton neighborhood has the highest number of Latinos by percentage (46.4 percent), followed by Brooklyn Center (29.1 percent), Stockyards (28.6 percent), and Ohio City (17 percent).

However, Cleveland does not have the highest percentage of Latinos in Cuyahoga County; that's tiny Linndale at 19 percent and Brooklyn at nearly 16 percent.

Of course, Cleveland is not the only Northeast Ohio city with a sizable Latino population. In fact, the region is home to the two cities with the largest percentage of Latino residents: Lorain (28.6 percent) and Painesville (25 percent).

Though the Mexicans arrived first in Lorain, most of the Latino population in that city traces its roots to Puerto Rico. National Tube Company, then a major employer in the industrial town, recruited workers from the island after World War II. Though the steel production is greatly diminished, the Puerto Rican connection to Lorain remains strong. The devastation caused by Hurricane Maria in 2017 prompted more emigration.

In Painesville, the majority of the Latino population is Mexican, particularly from the state of Leon. The community got its start in the 1980s with migrant farm workers who came to work in the area nurseries. The immigrants are credited with reviving the city by opening businesses and actually increasing Painesville's population.

A community center

At 13 percent of the city's population, Cleveland's Latino community is overshadowed by the larger Black and White communities, but it is growing in numbers and influence. It needs its own hub, the way Asia Plaza anchors AsiaTown, said Jenice Contreras, executive director of the Northeast Ohio Hispanic Center for Economic Development (NEOHCED).

In 2022, NEOHCED announced a plan to fill that gap with CentroVilla25, a development on the site of a vacant warehouse on West 25th Street near Clark Avenue with kiosk-style micro-retail spaces, a commercial kitchen, a business innovation center, and co-working space, in addition to an outdoor plaza with a restaurant.

"It will be the first time we own something, something that we built, by us, for us," said Contreras, who added that she hopes the center will give the area's Latino community a focal point and symbol of its growing clout.

Why Are the Metroparks So Amazing?

Greater Clevelanders tend to have an understandably low opinion of their local governments.

Scandals, corruption, waste, poor performance, inadequate services—residents have seen it all from their officials and government bodies. We've practically been conditioned to expect the worst from our public servants.

And then there's the Cleveland Metroparks, probably the only governmental authority in Northeast Ohio that is close to being universally loved. Ask any Cuyahoga County resident to list the best things about where they live, and they're likely to mention the Metroparks.

No county resident is far from one of the Metropark reservations, which is one reason they're a convenient retreat for people looking for nature, recreation, and exercise. The system has grown far beyond simply providing a place to picnic and enjoy nature. It's now also where we dine, attend concerts, party, learn about nature, and enjoy a day at the beach.

Three acres and a dream

The Metroparks began with three acres of bottom land in the Rocky River Valley donated to the city in 1912 by brewer Leonard Schlather.

That was all it took for visionary planner William Stinchcomb to launch what would become one of the finest metropolitan park systems in the country. Most of the land is in Cuyahoga County, but the Cleveland Metroparks also has property in Lake, Lorain, and Medina counties.

One gem in the Emerald Necklace. *Jim Sweeney*

As expansive as it is, the Metroparks system still adheres to Stinchcomb's original vision of an "Emerald Necklace" of parks ringing Cleveland and connected by boulevards. Stinchcomb first proposed the idea in 1905 when he was the chief engineer of Cleveland city parks, but it went nowhere. Luckily, the man was persistent.

Cleveland formed a park board in 1912. However, park districts were not allowed to receive public funding until state law changed in 1916. Once county commissioners were able to allocate funding, the Cleveland Metropolitan Park District was formed in 1917. Stinchcomb, then county engineer, worked as a consultant for the district.

With Stinchcomb's master plan as a guide, the district moved quickly to acquire land. In 1920, it owned only 109 acres in and around Rocky River and Big Creek. By 1930, it had 9,000 acres in large, unconnected reservations from Huntington to North Chagrin, property that otherwise would have been lost to developers or industry. The Metroparks that year also partnered with the Cleveland Museum of Natural History to offer outdoor education programming. During the Great Depression, the Civilian Conservation Corps and Work Progress Administration built roads, bridges, and shelters in the parks, many of which are still in use today.

Growth mindset

The Metroparks has never really stopped expanding and has proven itself opportunistic in taking over property from other governments, notably the City of Cleveland. It also regularly adds trails and other amenities to its existing reservations. It has become an equal partner with other governmental authorities—county, city, and state—in realizing the dream of better connecting Cleveland's waterfronts to the community.

In 2021, Cleveland Metroparks won the Award of Excellence in Parks and Recreation Management from the American Academy for Park and Recreation Administration, the fifth time it's been so honored.

There are times when the Metroparks seems to be the only government body Greater Clevelanders trust to do the right thing. When the Metroparks took over management of Edgewater and other lakefront parks from the state in 2013, the improvements were immediate and drastic: The beaches were cleaned regularly, and the lifeguard stations were manned. Metroparks has gone on to add other improvements on the lakefront, including a new family play space and Edgewater Beach House.

The addition of Merwin's Wharf in Rivergate Park gave people not only a place to eat but public docks from which to launch kayaks and paddleboards in the Cuyahoga.

Political independence

Perhaps Cleveland Metroparks' success is because it is its own independent political entity. The district is not part of City of Cleveland or Cuyahoga County government and so is insulated from many of the influences that taint local politics.

Like every other county park district in Ohio, the Metroparks is governed by a board of commissioners, composed of three citizens who serve three-year terms without compensation. Board members are appointed by the presiding judge of the Probate Court of Cuyahoga County. According to Metroparks CEO Brian Zimmerman, that unique structure allows the district to hire the most qualified employees without regard to nepotism, patronage, and connections.

That also helps explain why the system has had only six directors in its 105-year history. With an average tenure of nearly eighteen years, directors have been able to pursue long-range planning and provide stable management.

"This isn't a political appointment; it's a performance appointment," Zimmerman said.

Whatever the reason, it's working.

Metroparks Assets

24,000 acres	8 golf courses	1 zoo
300 miles of trails	8 lakefront parks	
18 reservations	2 marinas	

Metroparks Accomplishments Since 2010

2010—Hires Brian Zimmerman as director

2011—Acquires Seneca Golf Course from Cleveland, its eighth course

2012—Begins conversion of Acacia Country Club in Lyndhurst to Acacia Reservation; opens African Elephant Crossing at Zoo; acquires Rivergate Park

2013—Leases six lakefront parks from Cleveland and the state

2014—Adds Whiskey Island and Wendy Park to Lakefront Reservation; begins Edgewater Live and Euclid Beach Live concert series; opens Merwin's Wharf and East 55th Street Marina restaurant

2016—Wins Gold Medal for Excellence in Parks and Recreation Management

2017—Celebrates 100th anniversary; opens Edgewater Beach House; adds water taxi in Flats

2019—Opens Euclid Beach Pier

2021—Wins Gold Medal for Excellence for fifth time; opens Wendy Park Bridge and Whiskey Island Trail

2022—Voters overwhelmingly approve a ten-year, 2.7-mills replacement levy

What's the Rock and Roll Hall of Fame Doing in Cleveland?

The list of cities with better credentials than Cleveland to be the home of the Rock and Roll Hall of Fame and Museum is a long one.

New York, Detroit, Chicago, Los Angeles, Memphis, New Orleans, San Francisco, Boston, Philadelphia, and Seattle are among those cities with stronger rock backgrounds and more impressive rosters of homegrown musical acts. There is no "Cleveland Sound," and the city never gave birth to a particular musical culture or movement.

So why is the Rock Hall here? The simple answer is that Cleveland wanted it more, campaigned harder, and spent more money than any other city in contention.

Cleveland credentials

Of course, Cleveland does have some rock 'n' roll cred.

The city's role in rock history is small but notable. Alan Freed, a deejay at Cleveland radio station WJW in the 1950s, is credited with being the first to popularize the phrase "rock and roll" on mainstream radio (although the phrase originated earlier, in blues music as a euphemism for sex).

Freed also promoted the first major rock concert, the Moondog Coronation Ball, on March 21, 1952, in Cleveland Arena.

On the bill were Paul Williams and the Hucklebuckers, Tiny Grimes and the Rocking Highlanders, the Dominoes, Varetta Dillard, and Danny Cobb.

In a sign of rock's future, the concert was shut down by authorities. More tickets were printed than the arena's actual capacity due to a printing error and counterfeiting. When an estimated

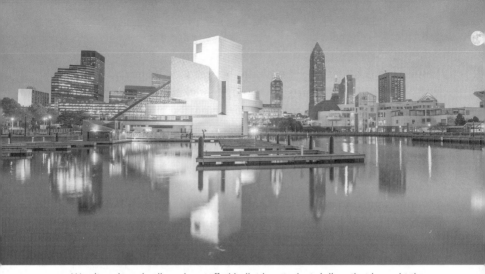

Was it rock-and-roll cred, a stuffed ballot box, or just dollars that brought the hall of fame to Cleveland? *fllphoto/stock.adobe.com*

20,000 individuals tried to crowd into an arena that held slightly more than half that, the fire marshall shut down the concert after Williams's first song.

Freed made an on-air apology the next day but was undeterred in his mission to popularize this new music. With the sponsorship of local record store owner Leo Mintz, the station gave Freed more on-air time to play his "race music." In 1954 Freed moved to New York City and rode the rising wave of rock and roll to movie appearances and even a TV show. However, a payola scandal derailed his career, and he later bounced from station to station. He died in 1965 at age forty-three from alcoholism.

Though Freed was originally buried in New York State, in 2002 his daughter-in-law brought his ashes to the Rock Hall, where the deejay is an inductee. The family later buried his ashes at Lake View Cemetery beneath a jukebox-shaped headstone.

While Cleveland developed a thriving rock scene and spawned a few national acts, it became known more for its enthusiastic crowds and its early support of nascent superstars such as Bruce Springsteen, David Bowie, and Rush.

In the 1970s, radio station 100.7 WMMS was one of the dominant FM rock stations in the country. Its deejays were local celebrities; studio appearances were a must for visiting acts; and the station helped break a number of national performers. Its buzzard logo was ubiquitous on T-shirts and bumper stickers. If you weren't a listener back then, it's hard to imagine now the power and influence the station had.

Building a campaign

The idea of building a hall of fame for rock and roll took root independently on both coasts during the 1980s. Famed promoter Bill Graham was planning one in his hometown of San Francisco. Atlantic Records founder Ahmet Ertegun and other industry executives formed the Rock and Roll Hall of Fame Foundation in 1983 with the intention of building the hall in New York City, original home to the recording industry.

Meanwhile, in Cleveland, Hank LoConti, owner of pre-eminent rock venue The Agora, had been pushing for a local museum to honor Freed and others. Ertegun's plans also caught the attention of K. Michael Benz of the Greater Cleveland Growth Association, the local chamber of commerce.

Benz realized the economic impact a Rock Hall could have on a city like Cleveland and assembled a team of civic and political leaders to pursue it. They enlisted Norm N. Nite, a well-connected New York deejay with Cleveland roots, to lobby for the new attraction to be built here.

The Rock Hall Foundation granted them an audience and, according to Benz, was blown away by the city's presentation. Up until that point, the New York group was more focused on the annual induction ceremony than the facility itself, which they intended to house in a brownstone donated by the city.

"I'm not sure they really understood what they had. In New York it's no big deal. In Cleveland it is," Benz said. "We waged a year-long campaign to land this. We were organized, we were tenacious, and we knew our stuff."

After visiting Cleveland in 1985, the foundation board decided to hold a nationwide competition. A number of cities bid for it, including New York, Memphis, San Francisco, and New Orleans, but it eventually came down to Chicago, Philadelphia, and Cleveland.

When *USA Today* in 1986 asked readers to vote on where the Rock Hall should be located, WMMS led a campaign that resulted in 120,000 votes for Cleveland, a runaway victory. The Growth Association followed with a 600,000-signature petition. The city even staged a Moondog Coronation Ball II in 1986, starring Chuck Berry.

Money talks

However, what really got the attention of the Rock Hall Committee was . . . money. The financial package that local and state authorities eventually assembled included $65 million for construction—more than Chicago or Philadelphia.

In May 1986, Cleveland was named the future home of the Rock Hall. Having won it, the city now had to decide where to build it. Possible locations included Public Square, the Flats, Playhouse Square, Mall C, Tower City, and spots along Huron Road behind Tower City.

Foundation officials settled on Tower City and hired famed architect I. M. Pei to design the building. However, when a record store opened in Tower City in 1990, the foundation nixed the site, claiming the store would cut into record sales at the hall. Eventually, officials settled on a city-owned plot on the lakefront at North Coast Harbor.

The proximity of Burke Lakefront Airport limited the height of the museum, but Pei delivered a signature building, including a glass pyramid reminiscent of the one he'd designed for the Louvre in Paris.

Finally in 1995, nine years after winning the Rock Hall, Cleveland celebrated its opening on Labor Day Weekend.

Location, location, location

The conflict between the foundation and city officials did not end with the opening, though.

Cleveland made an offer too good to refuse, but ever since then, the Rock Hall Foundation has given the impression of not being entirely happy the building ended up here. Notably, it refused to permanently locate the annual induction ceremony here, an unprecedented snub. After all, the NFL holds its annual ceremony in unglamorous Canton; Major League Baseball congregates in tiny Cooperstown, New York; and NBA immortals manage to find their way to Springfield, Massachusetts, every year.

While the Rock Hall opening in 1995 was celebrated with an all-star concert at Municipal Stadium featuring James Brown, Aretha Franklin, Bob Dylan, and Johnny Cash, the foundation did not automatically relocate the induction ceremonies, held since 1986, to the hall. In fact, Cleveland did not play host until 1997, and then not again until 2009. Through 2022, the inductions were held in New York City twenty-seven times, Los Angeles three times, and Cleveland six times: 1997, 2009, 2012, 2015, 2018, 2021. (The ceremony was canceled in 2020.) The foundation has said the ceremony will rotate between those three cities in the future.

Rock Notables from Northeast Ohio
(Hall of Fame members in bold)

Alan Freed	Dead Boys	Mushroomhead
Leo Mintz	Devo	**Trent Reznor (Nine**
Norm N. Nite	Eric Carmen and the	**Inch Nails)**
Bobby Womack	Raspberries	Pere Ubu
Bone Thugs-N-Harmony	**Joe Walsh and the**	Phil Keaggy and Glass
Bull Moose Jackson	James Gang	Harp
Chrissie Hynde (The	**Benjamin Orr (The**	Screamin' Jay Hawkins
Pretenders)	**Cars)**	The Black Keys
Cloud Nothings	Kid Cudi	The Moonglows
Dave Grohl (Nirvana	LeVert	**The O'Jays**
and Foo Fighters)	Machine Gun Kelly	Tracy Chapman
The Dazz Band	Marilyn Manson	
Rocket from the Tombs	Michael Stanley	

Who Is Slavic Village Named For?

Unlike Little Italy or AsiaTown, Slavic Village can leave outsiders wondering for whom the neighborhood is named.

Slavic Village is one of the oldest neighborhoods in Cleveland, but it has one of the newest names.

Formerly part of Newburgh Township, it attracted Irish, Welsh, and Scots immigrants who helped build the Ohio & Erie Canal and then worked in nearby mills. In the 1870s and 1880s, Czech and Polish immigrants arrived in the area. Commercial development flourished along Broadway and Fleet Avenues.

But it was two distinct neighborhoods, not a village. The Czechs called their enclave around East 49th Street "Karlin" after a district in Prague, the capital of the Czech Republic. The Poles called their area, centered on East 65th Street, "Warszawa" after the largest city in Poland.

So how did the Slavic Village name come about?

Marketing.

In the late 1970s, the neighborhood was in decline. Local attorney Teddy Sliwinski and his wife Donna were looking for a way to revitalize Fleet Street. They found inspiration just a few miles to the north in Cleveland's Little Italy, which was then reinventing itself as a local tourist attraction.

In 1977, the Sliwinskis and Kaszimier Wieclaw formed Neighborhood Ventures, Inc., to improve and brand the commercial stretch along Fleet into a more recognizable entity. Wieclaw designed distinctive Polish Hylander-style facades for many of the commercial buildings to provide a more uniform and identifiably "ethnic" look. A harvest festival (later renamed the Village Feast) was initiated to attract people from outside the area.

But the neighborhood needed a name. Naming it in honor of

Slavic Village Development Corp.

either the Poles or Czechs would have alienated the group that wasn't chosen. So they chose "Slavic" as a compromise. "Slav" refers to peoples in eastern, southeastern, and central Europe, including Russians and Ruthenians (eastern Slavs); Bulgars, Serbs, Croats, Slavonians, and Slovenians (southern Slavs), and Poles, Czechs, Moravians, and Slovaks (western Slavs).

Ironically, the name became best known during the foreclosure crisis from 2007 to 2010, which hit the neighborhood particularly hard.

"Back then, we used to joke that the name ought to be changed to 'Slavic Village the Epicenter of the Foreclosure Crisis,'" said Chris Alvarado, former executive director of the Slavic Village Development Corporation.

Not everyone embraced the renaming. One person living on Fleet Avenue hung a large banner on his porch reading "Waszawa not Slavic Village" after the rebranding.

And according to Alvarado, the name still isn't completely accepted. In a 2015 survey of residents, fewer than half identified their neighborhood as Slavic Village. And as the community has diversified, the name is less and less fitting. The community is about half Black now with a growing Latino population. At some point, Alvarado said, the community might have to reassess whether its name still fits.

Why Did Cleveland Neglect Its Waterfronts for So Long?

Northeast Ohioans visiting Chicago for the first time share the same reaction: Why can't Cleveland have a lakefront like this?

Grant Park, Lincoln Park, the Lakefront Trail, twenty-six miles of open and free lakefront, dozens of beaches, Navy Pier, and more—Chicago has embraced its waterfront while Cleveland for a long time treated its like an afterthought.

Though Cleveland owes its very existence to Lake Erie and the Cuyahoga River, its politicians, business leaders, and citizens ignored their recreational potential for most of the city's history. The city is in the enviable position of being located on the fourth-largest lake in the country, but planners over the decades declined to take advantage of this incredible asset. Indeed, they deliberately turned their backs on it.

It's only in the past few decades that planners have embraced the lake and river and begun the long, difficult, and expensive process of correcting more than one hundred years of development decisions that kept residents away from the water.

Lake Erie

One of the best views of Lake Erie from downtown is from the benches at the elevated northern end of Mall C. That vantage also shows everything that lies between downtown and the lake: an underused airport, an eight-lane interstate highway, railroad tracks, a seldom-used light rail public transit line, parking lots, a football stadium, private marinas, and more construction that effectively walls off downtown from the lake.

If the city had consciously decided to distance itself from the lake it couldn't have done a more effective job.

For much of the nineteenth and twentieth centuries, residents and civic officials viewed the lake as an asset, but primarily for industry and commerce, not for recreation or pleasure. The port was the hub of business, and railroads and roads were added to make the transport of goods easier and more efficient. The fact that much of downtown is built on a bluff overlooking the lake adds a natural barrier to the man-made ones.

Not surprisingly, planners viewed the sparsely developed lakefront as a convenient place to locate such necessities as railroad tracks and highways. When necessary, additional lakefront was created with landfill, though rarely for public use.

Piece-by-piece, structures were added: Municipal Stadium (1931), Memorial Shoreway (1930s), Burke Lakefront Airport (1947)—all assets for the city, but also additional barriers to the lake.

People who wanted to access the lake had to go west to Edgewater or east to Euclid Beach.

And because the public had limited interaction with the lake and river, it had become easy for them to be polluted by industry. So on the rare occasions when people did go to the lakefront, they found stench and dead fish on the beaches—making them unlikely to return. It wasn't until the ecology movement of the 1960s and 1970s that serious efforts were taken to save the lake and river.

Of course, not all the bad decisions were made by long-ago planners.

When the city sought a new NFL team after Art Modell moved the Browns to Baltimore in 1996, one of the league's requirements was a new stadium. The city, under pressure to build one quickly and on budget, took the easy path of putting the new First Energy Stadium on the same site as old Municipal Stadium. It might have been expedient, but it also guaranteed that a huge parcel of valuable lakefront property would be used only a handful of times a year.

Voinovich Bicentennial Park at the foot of East 9th Street was supposed to provide public access to the lake, but it has never

Passage of the Clean Water Act in 1972 began the process of reviving the Cuyahoga. It's still not always easy for people to use the river. *Jim Ridge, Share the River*

realized its potential. And while the Rock and Roll Hall of Fame and Museum and the Great Lakes Science Center do occasionally bring crowds to the lakefront, they don't encourage interaction with the lake itself.

There have been successes, however. The creation of Cleveland Metroparks' Wendy Park, with its birding trails and volleyball courts at the east end of Whiskey Island, and the 2021 construction of a pedestrian bridge over the railroad tracks to link Edgewater with Ohio City, helped join the lakefront, the riverfront, and a neighborhood.

The city continues to consider options for connecting downtown to the lakefront. Still, as much as access can be improved, significant barriers will remain for the foreseeable future: the East Shoreway is not going anywhere, and neither are the Norfolk & Southern railroad tracks.

The Cuyahoga River

If anything, the potential of the river has been neglected even more than that of the lake.

Until the 1970s, the portion of the Cuyahoga winding through the Flats and downtown was largely viewed as an industrial waterway and sewer, a means for transporting iron ore and cargo upstream to mills and factories and then carrying the waste and effluvia from those operations downstream back to the lake. The only people on the river or along its banks were those whose jobs or reduced circumstances forced them to be there.

The infamous 1969 "burning river" fire and the reinvention of the Flats in the 1980s as an entertainment district opened people's eyes to just how badly degraded the Cuyahoga had become, as well as the potential for what it could be.

Passage of the Clean Water Act in 1972 began the process of cleaning up the river, a remediation still underway but which has over time shown remarkable improvement. Pleasure boaters began to share the waterway with ore freighters.

But, as with the lake, reclaiming the riverfront from decades of neglect has been piecemeal and sporadic.

Public access to get on the river was virtually nonexistent until Cleveland Metroparks opened Rivergate Park and Merwin's Landing on the east bank north of Columbus Road. Before Merwin's public dock, kayakers and paddleboarders had to launch on Lake Erie at Wendy Park and paddle up the mouth of the Cuyahoga to reach the river.

With the exception of the Nautica entertainment complex, much of the riverfront development has been along the east bank. However, ongoing development of the Scranton Road Peninsula and the planned Irishtown Bend Park will go a long way toward transforming the west bank and connecting the Ohio City and Tremont neighborhoods to the river.

Irishtown Bend Park will complete the Cleveland Foundation Centennial Lake Link Trail, which connects Wendy Park on Whiskey Island to the 101-mile Towpath Trail extending south to New Philadelphia. A proposed residential complex on the west bank north of the river's original channel would add more residents and bring more activity to the river.

The city is finally reclaiming its waterfronts, which will improve the quality of life of everyone and make Cleveland a more desirable place to live, work, and visit.

What's So Special About Shaker Heights?

Shaker Heights is the Cleveland suburb most widely known outside our region.

Though neither the largest nor oldest suburb, Shaker Heights has a unique history: It's been a religious commune, a planned community for the well-to-do, one of the wealthiest cities in the U.S., a Jewish enclave, and a model for integration and race relations.

Shaker has never grown naturally or by accident but has followed various blueprints designed to create the ideal community.

Longtime resident Virginia Dawson, while writing a book about Shaker, spent a lot of time pondering what makes the city unique. "I wish I could figure it out, too," she said. "I think it has to do with being a planned community and all the work that went into its planning and all the resources that were lavished upon it."

The Valley of God's Pleasure

The first Shaker planners were trying to create paradise on Earth.

The community began in 1822 as the North Union Shaker Community, founded by The United Society of Believers in the Second Appearing of Christ, who also called their settlement "The Valley of God's Pleasure."

The Shakers were an offshoot of the Quakers, a Protestant sect that formed in England. Pacifist by nature, they were persecuted for their belief that people could gain direct knowledge of Christ without the benefit of clergy or creed.

The Shakers practiced communal living and shared all property. They didn't believe in procreation but relied on adoption and conversion to grow their ranks. They espoused gender and racial equality, separation of the sexes, and preached simplicity in dress and speech.

The Valley of God's Pleasure got its start when an early settler in the area travelled to Lebanon, Ohio, and visited a Shaker settlement there. He claimed to have had a vision during his trip home. His entire family converted and started the commune.

Undistracted by sex or other worldly pleasures, the Shakers were quite industrious, farming, producing natural remedies, and breeding livestock. The settlement grew to more than 1,300 acres and more than sixty buildings.

Of course, a commune whose members do not believe in procreation is not likely to prosper for long. After reaching a peak of about three hundred, the settlement's population declined after the Civil War. In 1888, those remaining sold the land to developers and moved to other Shaker communities. The sect's legacy can be seen in the Shaker Lakes, two connected ponds formed when the Shakers dammed Doan Brook to power their industries.

The Van Sweringen Brothers

After the Shakers' planned community failed, a remarkable pair of brothers set out to build a city according to their own ideal.

Oris Paxton Van Sweringen and Mantis James Van Sweringen were eccentric visionaries. Neither married. They lived together their entire lives, spending that time building an enormous fortune in real estate and railroads.

In 1905 the Van Sweringens set out to create the largest and wealthiest subdivision in the country on the site of the former Valley of God's Pleasure, which they renamed Shaker Village as a reference to the commune it replaced.

The brothers were determined to make Shaker special and exclusive. A typical north-south, east-west street grid would not do; instead, they laid out a city of curves, loops, and ellipses. The Van Sweringens dictated everything about their model suburb: where

The Shakers' planned community failed, but the Van Sweringen brothers' succeeded. *Spencer, via Wikimedia Commons / CC BY-SA 2.5*

businesses could be located, all architectural plans, minimum and maximum home costs, even approval of who was allowed to buy a home.

A 1924 ad for the new development promised "restrictions against all controllable community offenses" and "censorship of all building plans." It ended with the entreaty: "If you want a home where your children's companions are from equally well-ordered homes—find it here."

To lure wealthy residents from Cleveland, Shaker needed a public transit link to downtown, where those people worked. The brothers acquired the right-of-way through Kingsbury Run ravine (later made notorious by the infamous "Torso Murderer") and built the Shaker Electric Express (later known as the Shaker Rapid Transit, or Rapid). Desiring a better train station in Cleveland, the brothers turned a squalid ghetto south of Public Square into the gleaming skyscraper known as Terminal Tower (now Tower City) that remains downtown's most distinctive building.

The Van Sweringens lost their fortune in the Great Depression, and both died by 1936. But their vision for the suburb they'd built survived.

The Jewish capital of Ohio

By now, Shaker was home to Cleveland's leading citizens. The mansions along South Woodland and Shaker boulevards were the finest in the area and had replaced Millionaires' Row as the most desirable address. Its stately, tree-lined streets were used by the "right sort of people." But that prosperity had a dark side. Along with strict zoning and architectural requirements, the Van Sweringens had put in place property deed covenants designed to keep Jews, Blacks, Catholics, and other minorities out.

Because the covenants did not cover the entire suburb, the Jewish population was able to grow to 15 percent by 1937. The first synagogue in Shaker opened in 1957. The community increasingly became a destination for Jews moving from Cleveland's Glenville, Kinsman, and Hough neighborhoods. Eventually, Shaker, along with neighboring Cleveland Heights and University Heights, became the largest Jewish enclave in Ohio.

Even though more Jews now live in Beachwood than in the Heights, Shaker Heights still has a large and vibrant Jewish community.

Model of integration

When a Black family began to build a home in the Ludlow neighborhood of Shaker Heights in 1956, the house was firebombed. The violence shocked the city and forced a self-examination: Did Shaker want to experience the White flight that other suburbs were undergoing, or could it find a way to integrate peacefully?

The community chose the latter route. Although founded by the Van Sweringens as a racially and ethnically exclusive enclave, the city decided to become the opposite: the model of an integrated, prosperous suburb.

Shakerites formed the Ludlow Community Association and other neighborhood organizations to welcome Black residents as well as recruit new White residents to replace those who'd moved out. They battled predatory real estate agents and pushed banks to lend to both Blacks and Whites looking to move into Shaker.

The city even banned "For Sale" signs on lawns in order to combat White flight.

"Their belief was that the community was worth saving," Virginia Dawson said.

The Shaker Heights school district, the pride of the city, began voluntary busing in 1970 in order to integrate its schools. In the 1980s, the district closed several elementary schools and redrew boundaries to maintain integration.

While Shaker has managed integration better than most suburbs, it hasn't been without problems. In the 1970s, the city erected traffic barricades on six streets bordering predominantly Black Cleveland and Warrensville Heights neighborhoods. Shaker insisted it was to manage traffic, but Black residents on the other side of the barriers protested that it was to keep them out. The ensuing legal battles reached the Ohio Supreme Court, which generally sided with Shaker. Two of the six barriers remain today.

In recent years, achievement gaps between White and Black students in Shaker's public school system have sparked controversy and fueled racial tension. That friction made it an ideal setting for the bestseller and miniseries *Little Fires Everywhere,* by author Celeste Ng, who spent her teen years in Shaker.

So how well has Shaker Heights succeeded in its goal of becoming a model suburb?

According to the US census, Shaker Heights' 2020 population of 29,000 was 56 percent White and 35 percent Black. It had a median household income of $87,235, well above the national average, but also a poverty rate of 8.5 percent.

"People think Shaker Heights is a snobby, White, wealthy community, and it's none of those," Dawson said.

Whether Shaker can avoid the pattern of so many suburbs in which White residents move out and the suburb becomes majority Black remains to be seen. However, Dawson said she thinks Shakerites will fight to retain their unique status: "It's a community. People are involved. They like each other, and they like the place."

Shaker and celebrity

For a relatively small community, Shaker Heights has been home to a disproportionate number of famous people, particularly in arts and entertainment.

Because Shaker was home to a number of screen and TV writers, it's been referenced in a number of shows and movies. For example, Carter Bays, creator of *How I Met Your Mother*, made his real-life hometown the hometown of series protagonist Ted Mosby. It's also the home of Ward Cleaver, father on 1950s TV series, *Leave It to Beaver*. And it was the setting for the 2003 teen comedy, *The Battle of Shaker Heights*.

Here are some famous people who've lived in Shaker Heights:

Jamie Babbit (director, screenwriter)
Carter Bays (TV writer)
Andy Borowitz (writer, humorist)
Jim Brickman (musician)
Paul Brown (football coach)
Gary Cohn (president of Goldman Sachs and chief economic adviser to Donald Trump)
Kid Cudi (rapper)
Zelma Watson George (actress, singer, philanthropist)
Al Lerner (owner of the Browns and former chairman of MBNA)
Eddie, Gerald, and Sean Levert (singers)
Machine Gun Kelly (rapper)
Tommy LiPuma (music producer)
Lorin Maazel (conductor)
Paul Newman (actor)
Celeste Ng (writer)
Susan Orlean (journalist, author)
Harvey Pekar (cartoonist)

Roger Penske (businessman and race team owner)
David Pogue (science journalist)
Geraldo Rivera (journalist)
Molly Shannon (actress, comedian)
David Spero (deejay and music manager)
Reuben Sturman (pornographer)
George Szell (conductor)
Loung Ung (author and activist)
Oris and Mantis Van Sweringen (industrialists)
David Wain (actor, filmmaker, and comedian)
Kym Whitley (actress, comedian)
Fred Willard (actor, comedian)

What Was the Ohio & Erie Canal?

The bodies of water most often associated with Cleveland are the Cuyahoga River and Lake Erie, but if not for the existence of a third, man-made waterway, the community might never have grown into a big city.

In 1825, Cleveland, not yet thirty years old, was still a frontier town with a population of less than one thousand. It was growing, but the distance from the Eastern Seaboard was proving to be a problem.

That isolation posed a problem for the town's future. Farmers needed a way to get their crops to market, and settlers needed access to goods they couldn't produce locally. Overland travel on wagons was simply too slow (and railroads hadn't been built yet).

A route to the east

State officials turned to a solution originally proposed by George Washington: a canal between Lake Erie and the Ohio River. Such a waterway would allow a larger volume of goods to be shipped throughout the eastern half of Ohio (it had become a state in 1803) and points south, as well as provide another route to eastern markets.

For an example of the transformational power of a canal, Ohio political and business leaders had only to look at nearby New York, where the Erie Canal had just opened after eight years of planning and construction. The Erie Canal ran east from Buffalo to the Hudson River at Albany, which flowed south to New York City. It opened up the western frontier to further development as well as birthing a population boom in the region.

The canal helped Cleveland grow from frontier town to city. *Cleveland Public Library*

Cleveland merchants were now able to reach the Eastern Seaboard by shipping their goods to Buffalo and then through the Erie Canal. But a north-south connection to the Ohio River would benefit much of the rest of the state.

It wasn't a given that Cleveland would be the northern terminus of the proposed new canal connecting Lake Erie and the Ohio River. Painesville to the east and Lorain to the west were also contenders. The stakes were substantial; whichever city was chosen would secure its economic future.

Cleveland was selected largely due to the efforts of Alfred Kelley, a state legislator and the city's first practicing attorney. As a member of the commission formed to choose a canal route, Kelley successfully lobbied for his hometown.

Construction of the canal began in 1825. The 309-mile waterway was built in stages and, where possible, took advantage of rivers, starting with the Cuyahoga.

When it was completed in 1832, the Ohio & Erie Canal allowed cargo to move at 4 mph, the speed at which a team of mules could pull a canal boat. Goods could travel between the lake and river in the then-breathtaking time of eighty hours.

An economic boom

The impact was immediate. While other cities along the route such as Akron and Massillon benefited, Cleveland boomed. New businesses formed to handle increased trade on the port and river. Previously unavailable goods could be found on store shelves, and farmers planted more crops, confident that their goods would reach market. The canal accelerated Ohio's transformation from an agrarian frontier to an integral part of the nation's economy.

And the canal not only grew Cleveland's population; it diversified it. Up to that point, the settlers were largely transplanted New Englanders. But many of the Irish and German immigrants who dug the canal remained in the city and formed vibrant ethnic enclaves.

As transformative as the canal was, it did not last long. Within forty years it was made obsolete by railroads. Use of the canal fell sharply after the Civil War as it became faster and more efficient to travel and ship by rail. From 1904 to 1909 the state began rehabbing the canal, but massive flooding in 1913 destroyed many of the remaining locks and essentially ended it.

Remnants of the canal can still be found in Northeast Ohio. Bicyclists and hikers on the Towpath Trail in Cuyahoga Valley National Park can follow the former path and see the square-cut stones to which mules were tied. The Cleveland Metroparks Ohio & Erie Canal Reservation in Garfield Heights includes a visitors' center with displays and information about the canal.

Why Do Democrats Dominate Local Politics?

Ohio, once proudly purple, has been turning ever redder since the turn of the twenty-first century.

Ohio voted for Republican Donald Trump twice. After the 2022 midterms, the GOP had commanding majorities in the Ohio House and Senate and held all statewide elected offices except for one U.S. Senate seat.

But in this sea of red floats Cuyahoga County, an island of blue where Democrats dominate. Consider:

- Since Cuyahoga County adopted a charter form of government in 2009, all elected county administrators have been Democrats.
- The last Republican mayor of Cleveland was George Voinovich, who left office in 1986.
- Of the four congressional districts with chunks of Cuyahoga County, two are held by Republicans, but only because those districts also include large pieces of Republican-dominated territory in other counties.
- Registered Democrats outnumber registered Republicans in the county by more than two to one. In Cleveland, it's more than five to one.
- In 2020, Joe Biden won 66 percent of the vote in the county, even while Donald Trump won the state by 8 percentage points.

Why?

It's because of Cleveland. With very few exceptions, Democrats win cities. Virtually every big city, no matter where in the country, votes Democratic in national elections. A coalition of minorities, college-educated professionals, immigrants, young people, and union members carries the day for Democrats.

Democratic dominance in cities can trace its roots back to the early twentieth century when the rising workers' movement, largely populated by immigrants, allied with the Democratic urban political machines. Nationally, Franklin Delano Roosevelt built a New Deal alliance that included urban Roman Catholics and poor Southerners.

The Great Migration that brought large numbers of southern Black people to northern and midwestern cities also delivered an influx of solidly Democratic voters. The New Deal alliance didn't last, however. During the Civil Rights movement of the 1960s and 1970s, Republicans appealed to racist fears to pry away southern Whites.

The resulting urban versus rural divide persists today and, if anything, has become deeper.

Cleveland and, to a lesser degree, Cuyahoga County are strongholds of the New Deal Democrat alliance, said Mary Anne Sharkey, former politics editor of *The Cleveland Plain Dealer* and now a political consultant.

A large minority population, distinct ethnic communities, strong unions, and relatively low migration into the area combine to keep the region firmly Democratic, she said. It used to be gospel that a Democratic statewide candidate had to win Cuyahoga County by at least 100,000 votes to offset Republican gains downstate.

Could it change? Anything is possible.

After all, Mahoning County, home to Youngstown and once as reliably Democratic as anywhere in the country, voted for Trump in 2020.

Where Did That Suburb's Name Come From?

Ever wonder where Northeast Ohio communities got their names? Some were named after prominent local residents. Some for a local landmark or feature. Some were named after foreign cities. Others were variations on Native American words. Here's a rundown:

Akron—From a Greek word meaning "summit" or "high point." Fittingly located in Summit County.

Ashtabula—From the Algonquin word for "river of many fish."

Bentleyville—Named for Adamson Bentley, a local minister and merchant.

Berea—Named by a Christian congregation after the Macedonian city where, according to the Bible, apostles Paul, Silas and Timothy preached.

Bratenahl—Named after early settler Charles Bratenahl.

Brecksville—Named after the Brecks, local landowners.

Canton—Named for the Chinese city (but pronounced differently).

Chagrin Falls—Named for the Chagrin River waterfall. The river name is a modification of *Seguin*, the last name of a French trader who traveled in the area in the 1700s.

Elyria—Named for first resident Herman Ely.

Gates Mills—Named after sawmill operator Holsey Gates.

Lorain—Named after the county of Lorain, which was so named in tribute to the province of Lorraine, France. Previous names included Mouth of the Black River, Black River, and Charleston.

Medina—Named for a city in Saudi Arabia (but pronounced differently).

Oberlin—Named after Alsatian minister Jean-Frederic Oberlin. The college took its name from the town.

Olmsted Falls, North Olmsted, and Olmsted Township—Named after Aaron Olmsted, who bought the land from the Connecticut Land Company in 1795.

Orange—Named for the Connecticut town from which the early settlers came.

Painesville—Named after Edward Paine, a Revolutionary War general who settled in the area. Previous names included Oak Openings and Champion.

Parma—Originally named Greenbrier, the name was changed after a local doctor traveled to Parma, Italy, then led a campaign for the city to rename itself after the Italian city famed for its ham and cheese.

Pepper Pike—Unknown but thought to be named after either an early settler or the pepper trees that grew there. Pikes were privately funded toll roads.

Seven Hills—There are three theories: Named for the seven hills of Rome; named for seven local hills; or named after a notoriously hilly neighborhood golf course.

Shaker Heights—Derived from the North Union Shaker Community, which occupied the area from 1822 to 1889. "Shakers" was a derogatory term for members of the sect, who trembled and shook during worship.

Strongsville—Named for early settler John Stoughton Strong.

Vermilion—The town was named after the river, which had been so dubbed by the French for the reddish clay along the riverbanks.

Walton Hills—Named for early settler J. C. Walton.

Warrensville Heights—Named after early settler Daniel Warren.

Willoughby—Named by a local doctor and postmaster in honor of the president of the medical college he attended.

Acknowledgments

In the course of researching this book, I interviewed many people who generously shared their time and expertise about the city. I also spent a lot of time researching various sources of current and historical information. I am grateful for the institutional knowledge of the Cleveland Public Library, the Cuyahoga County Public Library System, Western Reserve Historical Society, the Cleveland Plain Dealer, cleveland.com, Cleveland Magazine, Case Western Reserve University, and Cleveland Historical, among others. I found the following books particularly helpful:

Cleveland: A Concise History, 1796-1996, Second Edition, Carol Poh Miller and Robert A. Wheeler, Indiana University Press (1997)

Cleveland: A Metropolitan Reader, Edited by Dennis Keating, Norman Krumholz and David C. Perry, The Kent State University Press (1995)

Cleveland: An Essential Compendium for Visitors and Residents Alike, John J. Grabowski, Black Squirrel Books (2019)

Cleveland: A History in Motion, John J. Grabowski and Diane Ewart Grabowski, Heritage Media Corp. (2000)

Cleveland's Millionaires' Row, Alan F. Dutka, Images of America (2019)

Cleveland: The Best Kept Secret, George E. Condon, George T. Zubal and P.D. Dole (1967)

The Encyclopedia of Cleveland History, David D. Van Tassel and John J. Grabowski, Case Western Reserve University (1987)

Canal Fever: The Ohio & Erie Canal, from Waterway to Canalway, Peg Bobel and Lynn Metzger, The Kent State University Press (2009)

Housing Dynamics in Northeast Ohio: Setting the Stage for Resurgence, Thomas E. Bier, MSL Academic Endeavors eBooks (2017)

Truth and Justice for Fun and Profit: Collected Reporting by Michael Heaton, Michael Heaton, Gray & Co. (2007)